Birds, Dogs & Kangaroos

Edited by Greg Echlin   Foreword by Fran Fraschilla

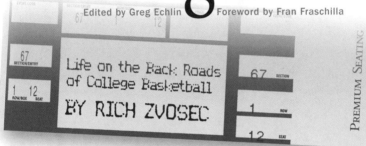

Life on the Back Roads
of College Basketball

BY RICH ZVOSEC

ASCEND
m e d i a

www.ascendmediabooks.com

Requests for permission should be addressed Ascend Media, LLC,
Attn: Rights and Permissions Department, 7015 College Blvd., Suite 600,
Overland Park, KS 66211.

10 9 8 7 6 5 4 3 2

Printed in the United States of America
ISBN-13: 978-0981716640
ISBN-10: 0981716644
Library of Congress Cataloging-in-Publications: Data on File

Book Design: Lorel K. Fox and Janine Taylor
Cover Design: Amber R. Leberman
Project Manager: Michael Lehr
Publisher: Bob Snodgrass
Editor: Greg Echlin
All Photos Courtesy: Rich Zvosec personal library unless otherwise noted

www.ascendmediabooks.com

Table of Contents

DEDICATION

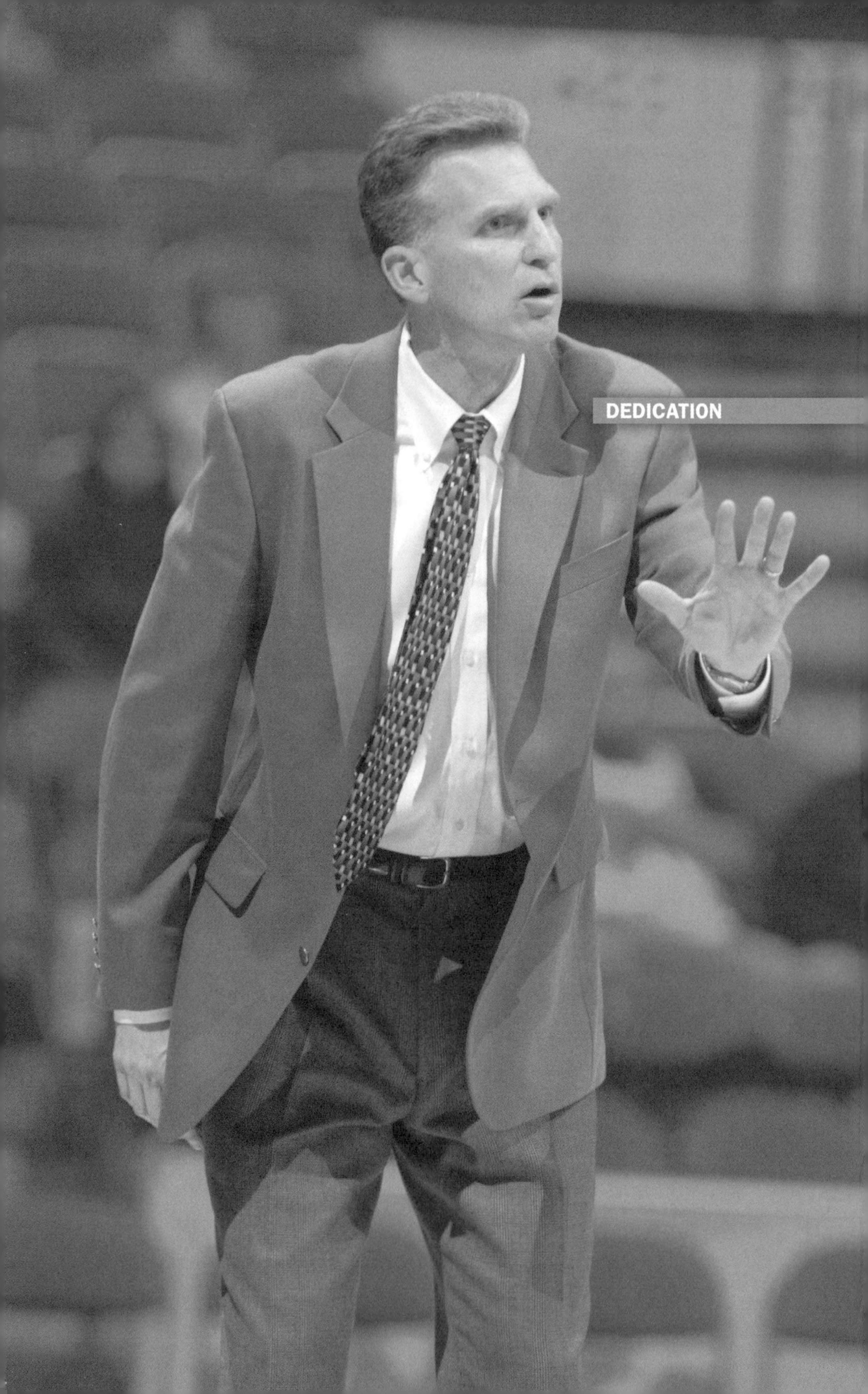

TO MY WIFE, SANDY, for her love and support that allowed me to chase my dream. I couldn't have done it without her.

TO COLIN, DEVIN AND KAILEY for all the joy you have given me.

TO MY MOTHER AND FATHER for giving me the belief that I could accomplish anything.

Acknowledgments

There are so many people I need to thank. I know I'm going to leave someone out, so I apologize up front.

I thank my wife Sandy who has stood by me all these years through the good, the bad and the many moves across the country. Being the wife of a coach means many nights alone, and worse, dealing with my post-game depression after a tough loss (or any loss for that matter). She's going straight to heaven for putting up with me. She is the most special person in the world. And to my children—Colin, Devin and Kailey—who have given me such great joy in watching them grow up. Your mother has done a wonderful job.

To my parents who always believed in me and supported me throughout the years.

I also want to thank the many coaches who influenced me along the way—Ken Weaver, John Williamson and Jim Lawhead. All of them helped me develop the love of the game.

To my college coach, Marv Hohenberger, who helped me get my first college job. And to Gary Edwards and Mark Amatucci who took a chance on a young coach and helped mold my philosophies. Also, I can't leave out a sincere thanks to Dean Demopoulos, Art Perry and Roger Blind, who weren't afraid to hire a former head coach and taught me you never stop learning.

Carlo Tramontozzi and Bob Thomas were two administrators who took a chance on a coach when everyone thought they should look elsewhere. To them, I'm grateful.

Thanks to all my former assistants and former players who made the ride so enjoyable. Guys like Ken Dempsey, John Rhodes, Jason Ivey, Che Roth, Jay Byland and Dwight Cooper were not only great co-workers, but true friends as well.

I owe a special thanks to Greg Echlin for editing this book. I haven't seen that much red ink on a paper since my sixth grade teacher returned my report on John F. Kennedy. And to the media savvy Roger Twibell who has been instrumental in my new career. Also, I would like to thank Mark Butler and Don Swanson for being the best friends a person could have.

Finally, thanks to the many parents and fans who have supported me through the years. There are so many of you. What a fulfilling feeling it was to have you backing me and giving me the opportunity to help your sons reach their potential.

Foreword

The social stratum in college basketball will always be on two different levels.

Schools like Kansas and North Carolina will always play in brightly lit, packed arenas and usually on national television, while St. Francis College, Sacred Heart and the University of Idaho will play in high school gymnasiums or empty arenas quieter than the school library. Powerhouse programs like UCLA and Kentucky will spend more on their media guides than some low major programs will spend on their travel budgets all season.

Duke University and USC will get hundreds of thousands of dollars worth of free basketball equipment for their student-athletes throughout the season. Fairleigh Dickinson University and Texas-Pan American will scrounge to make sure they have enough socks, sneakers and practice gear to get through the year. Plus, they will have to pay good money for them.

Dicky V and Billy Packer will follow the exploits of Texas' Rick Barnes and Florida's Billy Donovan closely throughout the year, but they might not be able to name the head coaches at the University of Maine and Centenary College. Wake Forest and Michigan State will eat some of their meals at Morton's and Ruth's Chris steak houses, while Rider will indulge in Golden Corral's '$7.99 special' with the all-you-can-eat salad bar.

BY FRAN FRASCHILLA

Most people who follow college basketball know about the big-name programs, the Hall of Fame coaches and the high school All-Americans who make a quick pit stop in college on their way to the NBA. Rich Zvosec brings to light a different side of college hoops. In fact, I guess you could say it is basketball from 'the other side of the tracks.'

It's safe to say you have probably never heard of Rich Zvosec. I am sure he won't be offended. But that probably makes him eminently qualified to tell the story of college basketball from the bottom looking up.

I have often said the No. 1 job title of a college basketball coach is 'crisis management coordinator.' Talk about managing crises. Zvosec's unique and amusing experiences at places the average basketball fan has never heard of will have you laughing out loud and shaking your head.

Birds, Dogs and Kangaroos will give you a greater appreciation for players and coaches at the low major level, who work just as hard— maybe harder—than the guys who come into your living room on ESPN during the winter. They take the losses hard and celebrate wins, often with a foot-long Subway sandwich for the long bus ride back to campus.

If you are a true college basketball fan, you need to know how the 'other half' lives, survives and sometimes thrives. Rich Zvosec will fill you in.

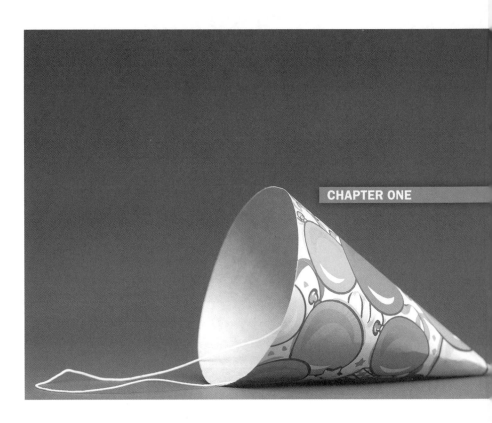
CHAPTER ONE

Happy Birthday. You're Fired.

"It is not the destination in life. It is the journey."

Those are the words I have lived by since I heard Basketball Hall of Fame announcer Dick Vitale speak at the Five-Star Basketball camp in Pittsburgh. I was a junior in high school at the time. My journey over the course of 25 years has seen me coach at ten different schools. If I were a player in the professional ranks, I would be referred to as a journeyman.

"We have decided to go in another direction."

The words anyone hates to hear most during a professional career. They are the most disingenuous words, in my case, a director of athletics can say. Tell me I didn't graduate enough players, I experienced too many off-court problems, or you just wanted to bring in *your* own guy to coach. But please don't insult my intelligence because no matter which scenario applies, it always comes down to winning more games. In college basketball, it's about winning and reaching the NCAA tournament. At the highest level, it's about winning the NCAA championship. Victories mean more revenue, more publicity and more students for the university. Universities will put up with low graduation rates, boorish behavior by coach and players— excuse me, student-athletes—and even some NCAA rules violations if the coach wins. Those are the facts for a college basketball coach.

March 13, 2007, was a day that changed my life forever. The fact that it was my 46th birthday was a weird twist of fate. I woke up that morning with a good feeling about the direction of the NCAA Division I basketball program I coached. Never in my wildest imagination did I figure how much a few hours later my life would change so dramatically. In fact, if there were any questions about my job security after a 12-20 season, I assured my assistants we were okay.

I even called Tim Hall, the new athletics director at the University of Missouri-Kansas City to let him know I could cancel a couple of recruiting trips if he wanted to move up the meeting. He said it wasn't necessary. Thus, I spent the previous five days on the road recruiting and put nearly 2,400 miles on my car. I even missed my 18th wedding anniversary to make a trip to Wichita. No way would my new boss let me do that if he planned to fire me, I thought.

Close to 11 a.m. I was set to meet with him. Hall was hired four weeks before our meeting. Though I didn't know him before the job search began, I felt good about the relationship we developed during his hiring process. Now, I thought, we were going to sit down for the first time, talk about the future of the basketball program and how we could take it to the next level. At UMKC, that meant winning a conference championship and playing in the NCAA tournament.

When I arrived a few minutes early, I found he wasn't alone. Sitting in his office was Doug Buchanan, the director of human relations. Not a good sign, I thought. As I sat down I could tell it was not going to be the type of meeting I anticipated. After superficial small talk between the three of us, Hall slid a piece of paper in my direction. Before I could read it, I heard the dreaded words, "WE HAVE DECIDED TO GO IN A

DIFFERENT DIRECTION." Those were words my friends and colleagues had heard, but never me. He then followed it up by saying, "BUT OF COURSE WE WILL HONOR THE TERMS OF YOUR CONTRACT."

"Big deal," I thought as I suppressed the urge to jump across the desk and send his head in a different direction. All I could get out was, "Of course you will honor it financially or our lawyers will talk, but you aren't really honoring it."

My final time out as head coach at UMKC.

It took only 15 minutes for my new boss to end what I spent thousands of hours building over the course of seven years, six as the head coach. And to think he was able to complete a full program review in less than a month. The irony was UMKC went 4-2 since his hiring. Plus we came within a jump shot of making the championship game of the Mid-Continent Conference (now renamed the Summit League) tournament for the first time in the program's history.

Buchanan took over the rest of the meeting and spoke more about the details and the terms of the contract. I interrupted Buchanan with a searing remark to Hall. I intended to take what I felt was the knife that was stuck in my back and turn it toward him.

"I wish the athletics director at Western Illinois had told me what type of person you were before he asked me to help you get the job," I blurted out. He stared into the distance without even acknowledging me.

As the meeting concluded I asked Hall one final question: "Would I have saved my job had I won the conference tournament?"

"Probably not," he responded.

"Yeah, right," I thought.

In my opinion, if I had won the tournament I could have named the number of years on my new contract. Knowing Hall worked for Sherwin-Williams before getting involved in college athletics, my second thought was, "I just got fired by a guy who was working for a paint company nine years before." At that moment a sense of calm came over me. As I walked out I knew I had an opportunity to either practice what I preached or wallow in the unfairness of it all. Get bitter or get better!

Moments later I was scheduled to meet with my team. They were my guys and would be forever. As I walked into the locker room, all of them were sitting and wondering what was going on. UMKC assistant athletics director for internal operations and senior woman administrator Cynthia Gabel (who unfortunately a few months later died of cancer) accompanied me. I guess Hall thought I needed a chaperone so I didn't say anything inappropriate. It was like a divorced parent being accompanied by a social worker when he sees his own children. To me that shows the ignorance of an athletic administrator who doesn't understand the coach-player bond. The relationship is like one of a father with his child. I have always looked upon my players as my sons, even after they were done playing for me.

My mind raced as I told the players the news. I wished them well and preached one more time about getting their academics done. I swore to myself I would not cry. It was hard. Midway through, I had to stop and regain my composure, but I believe the message was clear. I thanked them for their efforts through the course of the year and reminded them that I would always be there for them. After some hugs and final goodbyes, I was gone and resigned in my mind to know I was no longer the coach at UMKC.

Hard to believe it had been 20 years since my first head coaching job at St. Francis College in Brooklyn, New York. Now what?

CHAPTER TWO

Three Hall of Famers and A Kid

Most can tell you stories about life-changing experiences that put them on course for their line of work. For me it was when I was in eighth grade. My father was a high school coach in Elyria, Ohio, before he moved within the state to Lorain, a factory town whose biggest employers were U.S. Steel, the Ford Motor Company and the shipyards owned by George Steinbrenner. Although he never talked about having one of his sons follow in his footsteps, I could see the joy my dad got from the relationships he built with his players. My father always led by example. Two ideals he taught me were goal-setting and determining the formula for successful people.

With that thought in mind, I wrote three letters in 1975. To Bob Knight (Indiana University), whose Hoosiers went undefeated in the Big Ten that year and later at Texas Tech eclipsed the all-time record for college basketball victories; to John Wooden (UCLA), whose record of 11 NCAA championships in a stretch of 13 seasons is unmatched; and to Dean Smith (University of North Carolina), who was in the midst of guiding the Tar Heels to the NCAA tournament for 23 straight seasons. They were the best basketball coaches in the country, so why not write them? It didn't matter to me that they had no idea who this kid from Ohio was. My letter was short and to the point. It read like this:

Dear Coach Knight:

My name is Rich Zvosec and I am an eighth grader at St. Peter's School in Lorain, Ohio. I want to become a college basketball coach. What do I need to do?

Thanks,

Rich Zvosec

Within a month I received a letter from all three coaches explaining what I needed to do. All of them talked about getting an education. Along with Coach Wooden's letter, he sent me a copy of his "Pyramid of Success." (A few years later, when he spoke at the Lorain Sports Hall of Fame, he autographed it for me). Those three letters had a profound effect on my life. To think those great coaches would take the time to write me. I was walking on air. As I read and re-read those letters over the years, one other piece of advice came through—be ready to pay your dues! To a 13-year old from the Midwest, the only dues I knew were at the city pool and the library. I soon found out that wasn't what they were talking about.

Though their message wasn't forgotten, several years passed before I applied it.

On October 15, 1982, or thereabouts, we had finished basketball tryouts prior to the start of my senior season at Defiance College in Defiance, Ohio, when I was summoned to the office of the head basketball coach, Marv Hohenberger. Entering his office a couple of thoughts were going through my head, but as I found out, they were definitely different than what was going through his head.

I worked hard all summer on my game. I worked ten weeks of basketball camps across the country in preparation for that year. The camps enabled me to work on my skills while playing against some of the best players in the country. Future NBA players Ralph Sampson, Bill Laimbeer and Mario Elie were a few I had an opportunity to work out with. Little did I know how much it provided as a start to my coaching career.

Though I was not a great player, pretty average in reality, I felt I could be a contributor in my senior year with the Defiance Yellow Jackets. However, as I entered Hohenberger's office, I could tell by the look on his face he wasn't about to appoint me captain of the team that year. He was very direct as he told me I had a choice.

"You can sit on the bench in a shirt and tie and start your coaching career. Or you can sit on the bench in your uniform and never play," Hohenberger stated. Like most when told something they didn't want to hear I got defensive. More to the point I told him to shove it, or perhaps something a bit more colorful, and walked out of the office.

The next three days were a blur because I did what a lot of college students would do: Got drunk and cursed about how unfair the decision was. It took some coercing from my friend Don "Wink" Martindale (currently the linebackers coach with the Oakland Raiders) to help me see the light. He convinced me to go back and see Coach Hohenberger.

My first coaching job at my alma mater. Pay wasn't great (free), but the knowledge gained was invaluable. (Back row, 2nd from left.)

The next day I apologized for my outburst. To his credit Hohenberger never held it against me. I learned my first coaching lesson—never hold a grudge. I accepted his offer to become his assistant coach at Defiance.

During the year I learned a lot about keeping it simple and making bold moves. Coach Hohenberger was very good at taking offenses and defenses and breaking them down to their simplest form. It's no wonder he was inducted into the NAIA Hall of Fame after winning close to 600 games (581) at Defiance. He was not a yeller, yet he knew how to get his point across. I also learned as a coach you sometimes make decisions that are right, but not always popular.

Midway through the 1981-82 season, when we weren't playing well, he decided the two senior captains were not the leaders we needed. So he stripped them of their titles and made a freshman the team captain. Wow! How do you spell player revolt? But it never happened because he knew the freshman point guard earned the respect of his teammates. We went on to have a great season (21-10), advancing to the District 22 final (equivalent to a NCAA regional final). The district winner then advanced to the 32-team NAIA national tournament at Kemper Arena in Kansas City. En route to the district final, the Yellow Jackets knocked off Walsh College of North Canton, Ohio, coached by future West Virginia coach Bob Huggins.

As an assistant at Defiance, I also helped coach the junior varsity team. Besides that experience, I learned a few things about driving a van on the back roads in Ohio and Indiana. Coach Hohenberger designated me as the driver after our games. The operative word is 'designated' because shortly after we were on the road home he was fast asleep.

The drives were uneventful, except when I was assigned to drive the Taiwan national team to the airport. *That* was exciting.

Defiance played the Taiwanese in an exhibition game to kick off the season. The next day I drove the team to the Dayton airport. I'm not sure why I drove three hours to Dayton when either Detroit or Toledo was closer. About an hour into the drive the driver's side window shattered into a million pieces. It sounded like someone shot us with a gun. I never knew exactly what happened. All I remember were Taiwanese players speaking in rapid-fire chatter I couldn't understand. I asked the interpreter what they were saying. He told me they wanted to know if it was a terrorist attack and if they should hide under the seats. I told them to relax, or at least that's what I told the interpreter. I figured I should just keep driving as if nothing happened, so that's what I did the rest of the way to the airport. As they departed they thanked me as if I saved their lives. I quickly learned about the "glamour" jobs that awaited me as a college basketball coach.

When I reached college my biggest driving force was to become a college basketball coach. Sure, I wanted to play, but I could see my future before it happened. To that end I made a deal with Coach Hohenberger when he recruited me. If he helped me get a coaching position at a Division I college upon graduation, I would commit to the Yellow Jackets. He lived up to his word. After getting my degree in business education, I ended up at Bowling Green State University as a graduate assistant under Coach John Weinert in 1983. Of all the lessons I learned that year under Hohenberger, the two most important were how to manage people and fulfill promises.

Graduation day from Defiance College with my parents.

CHAPTER THREE

Camp Connections

Before moving on to Bowling Green, Ohio, I still had ten weeks of basketball camp to work. Every summer while in college I worked basketball camps in the Midwest and on the East Coast. I worked those ten weeks each summer at the best camps that would hire me for four years, including the summer after graduating from Defiance.

Working camps was the best way to meet coaches and learn about teaching the game. It was like attending a free clinic every day. Over the years I heard some great lectures from Jim Valvano, Digger Phelps, Dick Vitale, Terry Holland and Mike Krzyzewski to name a few. I met some great people and as an added bonus learned the business of running basketball camps. That knowledge became valuable during my coaching career because camp income helped pay a lot of bills through the years. Also, it was a lot more fun coaching and playing basketball all day than working in the steel mill back home.

In each of those four years my summer started off with a two-week stint at the University of Notre Dame. It was a tremendous thrill for me since I grew up a Fighting Irish fan. Digger Phelps, the coach of the Irish at the time, was a hands-off type of coach at his camp. He would have made a perfect politician. Besides being one of the best at shaking hands and kissing babies, he opened and closed the camp. At night he was always around talking with the coaches and answering any questions from us. It wasn't always the answer you wanted to hear because he didn't hesitate to share his philosophy. One time Phelps got a little heated when a high school coach from Florida asked why he let Brigham Young University guard Danny Ainge dribble the length of the court to beat them in the 1981 NCAA tournament. I think his answer was simply, "Pack your stuff." Next question!

He could be Dr. Jekyll one minute and Mr. Hyde the next. One summer he took the coaches who were working both weeks to his house on Lake Michigan for the weekend. Talk about history. The old house once belonged to the late legendary Notre Dame football coach, Knute Rockne. Everything went well—Coach Phelps grilled the steaks and handed out the beverages—until someone got the tram stuck. (That's right. The house had a tram that carried its occupants to a hilltop overlooking Lake Michigan). Suddenly it was like flipping a switch. He cursed everyone and threw our bags down the the hill. A couple minutes later, after we got the tram working again, Phelps went back to being the hospitable host.

Sitting there, talking strategy, was like receiving a graduate degree in coaching. It was also a chance to rub elbows with some other up-and-coming coaches. The list read like a who's who for an aspiring young coach: There was Pete Gillen, who went on to become a successful head coach at Xavier University before Virginia lured him away in the Atlantic Coast Conference; Jim Baron (Rhode Island); John Carroll (Boston Celtics); Jeff Nix (New York Knicks); and even the future athletics director at Seton Hall, Joe Quinlan. I mentioned Quinlan last because he became a link in my job search down the road. After my stint at Notre Dame, two weeks at Purdue followed, then off to the East Coast. There

I worked the next six weeks before heading home.

You might think every camp is the same, but each had its own unique feature. For example, the camp at Syracuse University drew 600 campers a week, all in one spot, the Carrier Dome. At Notre Dame and Virginia it was all about tradition. The Pocono (Pa.) Invitational Basketball Camp and the Holy Cross Crusader

Networking at Notre Dame camp. The paycheck I am holding barely covered my beer tab for the week.

camp in Massachusetts were moneymaking machines. The best teaching camp was the Mason Dixon camp run by Morgan Wooten, the legendary boys coach at DeMatha High School outside Washington, D.C. The toughest one to work, yet the staff was one of the best in the country.

Not only did the 40 weeks of camp in those four years provide me a great opportunity to learn and network, but the experiences also left me armed with stories to last a lifetime. One of the first camps I signed on with was the Pocono Invitational. The Kennedy family ran it. Not the political one, but rather the basketball family in New Jersey. Believe me, politics was still a part of that clan as well. They were tied into everything on the East Coast. Bob Kennedy, the owner-operator, and his brother Pat (the former head coach at DePaul, Florida State, Montana and Iona before taking over at Towson University) built a camp in the beautiful Pocono Mountains. Campers lived in cabins and ate in a mess hall while living their basketball dream for a week. Coaches did the same. In my first summer, I worked three weeks for $70 a week. I think, when it was all said and done, my beer tab was more than I made. I had to drink something to counterbalance all of the "bug juice" that was served with the meals. The Kennedys proclaimed "bug juice" as the elixir of life, but I knew it was just watered down Kool-Aid.

It was supposed to be instructional and fun, but sometimes the competitive juices got the best of the coaches. During my second day there, I watched two high school coaches from New Jersey get into a fight over the score. Great example for the kids, I thought, sarcastically. Though camps ended Friday, many of the camper's parents were on vacation until Saturday morning. That meant you had to be there until all the campers left. One week an aspiring young coach, Jay Wright, made a commitment to be in a Saturday wedding in Philadelphia. After being told he had to stay through Saturday or he wouldn't be paid, Wright took matters into his own hands. He had the campers from his cabin attack my cabin and pull out all the mattresses. Even back then he wasn't afraid of unconventional strategies. When fired, he left with a smile on his face. Now, as the head coach at Villanova, I doubt that he worries about that $70 he gave away.

Two of my favorite camps to work were the University of Virginia camp run by Terry Holland, who at the time was with the Cavalier program, and the Mason Dixon camp despite it being the toughest. The UVA camp was great because of its setting. Holland, one of the sincerest and warmest coaches I ever met, assembled a staff then that was just as helpful. Among them were Craig Littlepage (current AD at Virginia) and Jim Larranaga (who later coached George Mason University to the Final Four).

Like a lot of college camps, Virginia used its camp to recruit players and the Cavaliers brought in potential big-time players. At the end of the second week I was approached by Coach Larranaga, who asked if

I could drop off a couple campers in New York City on my way to the
Holy Cross camp. Little did I know whom I had in the car when we left
Charlottesville. Three guys piled into my car and we headed for the Big
Apple. I couldn't have imagined how much future money was in that
car. The three were Olden Polynice, who put in more than ten years
in the NBA; Mario Elie, a member of three NBA championship teams;
and Antoine Ford, who played for Bobby Cremins at Georgia Tech and
later professionally overseas. If I had any idea how successful those guys
would become, I would have asked them for some gas money. I dropped
them off in the Bronx about 3 in the morning. As I pulled out, I passed
a park packed with kids playing basketball. I made a mental note in my
mind, "Make sure to come back here to recruit." If I were in the movies,
I'd call that foreshadowing. I don't just mean coaching at St. Francis
College, where I eventually landed my first head coaching job, but all the
late night drives on the recruiting trail.

The Mason Dixon camp was the hardest to work because the players
received 12 hours of instruction. The only breaks we had all day were 30
minutes for lunch and 45 minutes for dinner. As the legendary former
Colgate coach, Jack Bruen, used to say during the slide drills, "step-slide,
step-slide, step over the cheese." Though we worked our tails off, the quality
of the staff and the camaraderie we developed made it all worthwhile.

In the first summer of the Mason Dixon camp, the following
speakers came in to talk: Coach Krzyewski, Valvano, Cremins, Gillen,
and Adrian Dantley. And that was the first week. I understood why they
came in and spoke for free. They had their eyes on Danny Ferry, the son
of former NBA player and general manager Bob Ferry. Danny's stock was
rising as a high school senior for Coach Wooten at DeMatha, so everyone
tried to get an edge. Coach K ended up landing him at Duke. Though the
speakers were great, the staff was better.

The coaches at Mason Dixon who supervised each of the "leagues" were called commissioners. Like the Notre Dame camp, it also read like a who's who list: Mike Brey (Notre Dame), Perry Clark (the former Tulane and Miami head coach), Jack Bruen (Colgate) and Pete Strickland (N.C. State) among them. Bruen, the commissioner of my league, turned out to be a great friend and one of the best people I ever met. He had a way of getting people to give a little bit more, even when they didn't think they could. That's why he was such a great coach.

There were some hard partying nights along the road. The most enjoyable nights on the road were when a bunch of us got together and talked hoops. With a few beers the strategies really flowed. One of the best places to do it was at the Ott House in Emmitsburg, Maryland. That's where Bruen, now deceased, held court for two weeks during the Mason Dixon camp. Not only could he talk basketball, but he knew the words to every song on the jukebox and wasn't afraid to lead the band of coaches. Before Colgate, he was the head coach at Catholic University in Washington, D.C., and also made a living in the District tending bar at Jack Baker's. From him I learned early on that if you want to hoot with the owls at night you had to be able to fly with the eagles in the morning. I followed Bruen's lead of drinking Coke like it was water to pump in the caffeine. Six chocolate donuts and a 32 oz. Coke can really jumpstart the heart.

That camp also provided me with the introduction to two coaches who had a major impact on my career and became lifetime friends. Mike Voyack was an assistant coach at Hofstra University, and Bob Valvano had just left the Hofstra staff to become the head coach at Kutztown University in Pennsylvania. (Yes, he is the younger brother of the late Jim Valvano, who led North Carolina State to the 1983 NCAA championship. That's a question I am sure Bob has answered hundreds of times). Voyack and Valvano worked with Gary Edwards, a new hire as the head coach at Atlantic Christian College (now known as Barton College) in Wilson, North Carolina. That became a big key to my future.

In '83, my coaching future took a big step at Bowling Green under John Weinert. In so many ways, it was the greatest learning experience I could have as a young coach. The 1983-84 season with the Falcons was about doing as much as I could with hopes of moving up on the staff. I worked with a fine group of assistant coaches there, with Bruce Brown as the lead assistant, who were very organized and always intent on improving a player fundamentally. Weinert was very much a Bob Knight disciple, right down to wearing the same type of red plaid jacket Knight used to wear in the '70s at Indiana.

Check out the coaching outfit at Bowling Green University.

Unfortunately for Weinert, instead of the red that's associated with the Hoosiers, the Falcons' colors are brown and orange. Ron Johnson was the other assistant, a great guy who played for Coach Weinert at St. Joseph's College in Rensselaer, Indiana. He was more of a laid back personality who was good at playing off Bruce. The other coach on staff was Steve Williman, a graduate assistant like me. A successful high school coach, he was working on his master's degree at the time with hopes of moving further into college coaching. Steve and I had some real heart-to-heart talks that year and he became a good friend. At the end of the year he decided to go back to high school coaching. Since then he has one state title and one runner-up finish to his credit in Ohio.

In those days, being a graduate assistant meant you had other duties besides coaching. For me it meant teaching data processing. Also, I was assigned to a professor in the business education department. The class usually had about 20 female students and four or five males (athletes most of the time). It proved to be very beneficial because the head of the department, Dr. Dave Hyslop, doubled as the faculty athletic representative. For all of my duties, I was paid $4,500 for the year. The only affordable place for me to live was in an apartment above a garage. Since I wasn't there much, except to sleep and shower, it didn't matter. A typical day went as follows:

8:00 a.m.	Teach class
9:00 a.m.	Work in basketball office
3:00 p.m.	Practice
6:00 p.m.	Attend graduate classes
9:00 p.m.	Make recruiting calls until midnight

It was quite the juggling act. However, what I looked forward to the most was phoning the recruits. The best time to talk with guys was after 9 p.m. because high school kids are hardly ever home before then. The conversations varied, but always steered back to Bowling Green being the perfect fit for the player. Some players talked more easily than others, but the goal was getting them to feel comfortable with you. Often times I listened to a recruit's problems with a girl or how his parents didn't understand him. Because I was so close to their age, I felt I related better than most and in the end built some great relationships. Even though many of them never attended Bowling Green.

The year at Bowling Green went fast, and I learned quite a bit of what to do and not to do. Coach Weinert was a very good game coach, but didn't seem to care much for practice. In fact, during most practices Coach Brown would run the fundamental drill sequences while Weinert stood to the side. Occasionally he would pull a player off, give him some instructions, then tell a joke. He loved to do that at the oddest times. At first I leaned over to hear what he was saying, but when I realized it was the same joke, I tuned out. I never understood the purpose, but picked up some pretty good jokes.

As the low man on the staff I had some jobs some would think are beneath them. I did, too, but I remembered the piece of advice from the three Hall of Fame coaches about paying dues.

One job was to keep the Slurpee machine working. Coach Weinert was very proud of the fact that only Indiana and Bowling Green had a Slurpee machine in the locker room. I wasn't. It took me only a week to break it and a whole year for the part to be ordered and delivered. So much for my duties as a Slurpee delivery boy.

The other job was to pick up players at the airport. Most of the time the players were grateful for the ride, but some guys were a pain in the ass. One player always flew into Detroit because it was less expensive, meaning it took me an extra hour each way, and never said thank you. On top of it all the guy was a stiff. I filed that away for future reference as I recruited kids—decide on their character.

Two incidents stick out most in my mind that illustrated the coaching ability, and quirkiness, of John Weinert. In a game at Boston University with three minutes to go in the game, we were down by five. Weinert called a timeout and put in a full court press. That's not that strange, except that we had not practiced it. The next thing I knew we stole the ball three times and won by three. As we walked off the floor I learned a valuable lesson on getting players to do what you want them to do.

A month later we played at the Lobo Invitational in Albuquerque, New Mexico. The games were played in The Pit, where Jimmy V had his greatest moment in '83. The arena name describes how the court is set, below the stands, giving a great home court advantage to the Lobos. As part of the tournament all the coaches were required to talk at a luncheon. Each coach was expected to get up, talk a little about his team and praise the tournament organizers. Not John Weinert. His first line was that Mexican food was his second favorite thing in the world after a root canal. Dead silence. All I could do was continue to eat and hope nobody noticed the Falcon blazer I wore. When the luncheon ended we made a beeline exit to avoid any confrontations. The next day we went out and slipped by California, 59-58. But on the last day of the tournament we lost a 12-point lead in the second half to the home team, the University of New Mexico. The Lobos ended up winning by a dozen, 86-74. Can you spell home cooking? Now I know why they call it The Pit.

The rest of the year was a clinic in recruiting organization and how to work the phones. I really enjoyed talking to recruits about Bowling Green and coaching in Anderson Arena, better known as The House That Roars. My juices got going when I knew we were in for a recruiting battle. Per NCAA rules, I was permitted to write and call recruits, but I couldn't recruit off-campus. My desire to recruit off-campus meant it was time to move on at the end of the season.

In the spring of '84 I drove to the Columbus, Ohio, airport to meet my future boss, the previously mentioned Gary Edwards. My friendships with Mike Voyack and Bob Valvano at the Mason Dixon camp helped me get my foot in the door with Edwards, who had just been hired at Atlantic Christian College, a NAIA school that later moved up to NCAA Division II. It was time to finish the deal.

CHAPTER FOUR

Losing a Car But Getting a Job

I was scheduled to meet Edwards at the airport in Columbus because he was passing through on an airline connection for a recruiting trip. My big chance. The vision of a full-time coaching job. I parked my car and went inside to meet him. Then, when we went back, the car wasn't there. Here I was trying to make a good impression and I thought someone stole my car. We walked around for about 30 minutes until it dawned on me that there are two sides to the airport. We went out the wrong side, so after crossing over to the opposite side, we found my car. That was the good news. The bad news was my time ran out and Edwards had to make his connection. After talking about what I could bring to the table, we shook hands and he was gone. So was my job. That's what I thought anyway.

In the meantime, I had an interview with Tom Chapman, the head coach at Gannon University in Erie, Pennsylvania. Coach Chapman kept repeating during the interview, "You need to bring me players to help keep food on the table for my family." The fact that Chapman weighed more than 350 pounds at the time prompted me to think, "If you ate less, your family would not have to worry." Needless to say, I didn't feel good about a job offer. But a week later Coach Edwards called and fortunately offered me the job as an assistant at Atlantic Christian. I was on my way to North Carolina the following day.

Atlantic Christian College was a long way from the better known ACC (Atlantic Coast Conference), but I was as excited as if I had landed a job at the University of North Carolina in Chapel Hill. Upon arriving in Wilson, I hooked up with Dave Jauss, the new baseball coach at the time and now the bench coach for the Baltimore Orioles. We became roommates and shared an office.

I had a dual title—assistant basketball coach and director of intramurals. My pay almost doubled as I made the "princely" sum of $8,100. I looked at my job as strictly a basketball coach while the AD, Bruce Curtis, thought I was the intramurals director. At times we banged heads, but I lived my dream as a college basketball coach. That's what registered most.

My main responsibility was recruiting. However, as the only assistant, I did a little bit of everything. A short list was painting the weight room, washing uniforms, promoting the program and checking on academics. Somewhere down the line I did some coaching. Pretty glamorous!

My first shot as a full time assistant at Atlantic Christian College. Oh yeah, I ran the intramural program as well.

In the first couple of weeks I set up the intramural schedule which included the Great Tin Can Giveaway, a contest in which fraternities and sororities collected empty cans to win gift certificates donated by local businesses. I then took the cans and exchanged them for cash. At that time I could use the cash. And the students received free meals from local restaurants.

Another task I started was painting the weight room and the gym in an attempt to change the mentality of the program. "A fresh coat of paint wouldn't hurt," I thought. Then one day Coach Ed Cloyd, ACC's longtime golf coach, informed me I was not following the color code of the building. I figured since it hadn't been painted in more than 25 years that no one would mind. I guess you can't please everyone.

Most challenging was the recruiting chase. Knowing we were going to bring in a whole new team, it was a great opportunity to make my mark. Coach Edwards's idea of recruiting players was simple: Bring in the best player, and we'll figure out the rest later. "Anywhere, anyplace, anytime" was our motto in recruiting. It meant that I was on the road for the better part of a year. My first recruiting trip covered about 6,000 miles through the Midwest. The AM radio in my car became my best friend.

My bags were packed and my maps were ready. I put together a presentation of the school that included a slide show. Over the next three weeks I became a traveling salesman. My first stop was Roanoke, Virginia. Unfortunately, I took a wrong turn and ended up being two hours late. I was so nervous as I gave my first recruiting pitch that I started to eat the peanuts in the bowl in front of me. I ate half of them before the player's mother informed me his grandmother liked to eat only the chocolate candy coating off them, but leave the peanuts. I left the other half for someone else. Not a very good beginning.

From there I headed north to Ohio, Indiana and Illinois. During one stretch of two days I watched nine games in three different states (six in Illinois, two in Indiana and one in Ohio). By the time I returned to North Carolina I had a list of 25 solid high school prospects with varied interest in our school. We didn't sign one of them.

After telling Coach Edwards all about those fantastic players, he said two words I'll never forget, "Junior college!" His point was my first trip was an opportunity for me to get my feet wet and practice my recruiting pitch. Since we sought players who could help us immediately, it meant signing primarily junior college players. So that's what we did. Of the ten players we signed, all but two were either transfers or junior college players.

Each player came with his own story, and all of them made an impact on the program. Michael White was the first player brought in. He was a 6-foot-9 man-child from Brooklyn, New York. We discovered him at a recreation center in Coney Island. He joined us at midyear, but never played. I tried like crazy to help him get eligible, but he couldn't pass Human Sexuality. To think he referred to himself as "Sweet Meat." He did, however, provide me with one of the most interesting nights of my life.

I was bound for New York on a recruiting trip, so I took him with me. That way he could visit his family. After dropping him off and watching a game at Christ the King High School, I headed back to Brooklyn. Figuring I'd get a hotel for the night, then leave in the morning, I didn't count on the exorbitant cost of a hotel stay. Finally, I found a hotel that charged for half-night stays in Sheepshead Bay. It was perfect because it wasn't too far from where Mike stayed. When I checked in I thought it was strange they asked for cash up front. Then I discovered after entering my room that the walls were a little thin. I could hear everything. And I mean everything. People were definitely enjoying themselves. As I walked out the next morning with my bag big enough to carry a body, I realized I spent the night in a hotel primarily used by prostitutes. Since I was alone, the clerk must have thought I had an inflatable doll in my ACC bag. I swear I didn't!

On the way back I stopped at Mercer County Community College in West Windsor, N.J., to see its team practice. I had met the head coach, Howie Landa, at a Five-Star camp a few years earlier. He was a coach there when I was a camper. We struck up a friendship and stayed in touch through the years. A terrific coach and a great guy, he had just the player for us. His name was Ed Boone. One problem: Ed was ineligible and wasn't able to play the rest of the year. He told me to come back New Year's Eve when I could see him in a scrimmage. Good. I knew what I was doing for the holidays.

During the 1984-85 season I made weekly trips to the Baltimore-D.C. area to recruit. That meant after practice Friday driving five hours to catch a game Saturday, then a Sunday afternoon game in Baltimore. On a good weekend I could pull off the hat trick: See a junior college and high school game on Saturday, then go to a Baltimore Catholic League game the next day. Our budget wasn't that big, so it meant crashing with a friend and eating a lot of fast food. The only expense was gas. Hell, I couldn't even afford to turn in the mileage.

On one of my drives home I heard an interview on the radio with former Kentucky assistant Joe Dean Jr., who had been hired as head coach at Birmingham-Southern. The interviewer rambled on about how hard Dean worked at UK. While other passengers slept on the Wildcats plane flight home, Dean was busy writing notes. Hard work. Right. Try writing notes while driving down I-95 in the middle of the night. I compiled almost 60,000 miles on my car that year, but my training and the recruiting stories that went with it made it priceless. I lost count of the number of notes I wrote while driving.

The trips to Baltimore paid off with the commitment of a point guard and a 6-foot-9 center from the Community College of Baltimore County (CCBC). Unfortunately, the player we really wanted wound up at Kentucky Wesleyan. He owed money and couldn't get his transcript released. There was no way I could have lent him the money based on my bank account at the time. Besides, I wanted to do anything to get a player, but breaking rules was not an option.

"Doing anything" took on a new meaning when I went to see a player by the name of Ricky Henry. He was a transfer who actually visited our campus on a weekend when we were on the road. In fact, he played some pick-up games with our players before a security guard threw him out for not being a student at the school. So there I was trying to get an evaluation of him and at the same time convince him the guard was just doing his job.

As I drove up to his house in Wilmington, Del., I was sweating buckets. The car I bought before I moved to North Carolina didn't have air conditioning. Smart move! The only way I could evaluate him was by seeing him play, so with a park across the street from his house I suggested we get a game going. We rounded up seven guys including his brother, Rodney and their friend Darwin Purdie (both of whom eventually played for me at St. Francis). We were one player short, which meant I had to play. There was only one problem. All I had with me were the dress clothes I wore (this was supposed to be an up-and-back trip), but I had sneakers in the trunk. So there I was playing in the same clothes I wore to church. They must have thought I was nuts when I dove for the loose ball (old habits are hard to break). I would like to think my willingness to play in my dress clothes sold Ricky on why he should play for us at ACC. And he did.

The final piece to the recruiting puzzle was Ricky Melendez. He was a kid I grew up with in Lorain, though he was a couple of years younger. Melendez went to work out of high school as a night manager of a convenience store, then realized he should consider college when a robber pulled a knife on him over a can of Spam. By the time I arrived at ACC, he had developed into an all-conference player at Lakeland Community College in Willoughby, Ohio. Though numerous schools recruited him, I felt he trusted me. He played on my summer league teams during high school. As we went to meet his mother, I told Coach Edwards that it should be a slam dunk if he didn't say anything to antagonize her. Two minutes into the conversation he took a shot at Gannon University. Erie, Pa., was closer in proximity, so it was easier for Ricky's mother to see her son play there. But Coach Edwards put it less than tactfully: "She would need to follow a snow plow up there because of the weather." For some reason that set her off, so I had to drag Coach Edwards out to prevent him from being struck by a frying pan. Ricky followed us outside assuring us everything was okay. He said he would come on one condition—we had to get his girlfriend into school. Consider it done, I told him, so he became the last addition to the program. As we walked away Coach Edwards asked how I knew we could get his girlfriend into school. I figured if we could get him into school, it would be a snap since she was tutoring him.

Bringing kids in for a visit proved to be an adventure as well. Unlike BCS schools that fly their recruits in on private planes, we used People Express. Or I drove them to campus. If you don't remember People Express, in business from 1981 to '87, let me refresh your memory. It was the airline than resembled a bus line in the sky. You paid for your ticket on board as the flight attendant rolled his or her cart down the aisle like a train conductor. The prices were great, but there was one catch. You had to connect in Newark, New Jersey. That was okay if you were flying from Boston, or even Pennsylvania, but if you were flying from Baltimore, it didn't make too much sense. We flew in a couple recruits and for the most part I was the one picking them up.

Sometimes I caught a break. Once I picked up two prospective players from Virginia Beach (about a three-and-a-half hour ride), so the ACC vice president lent me his Lincoln Town Car. Little did he or I know the return trip would be somewhat longer in distance. At the end of the visit one of the players informed me that he had to go back to his junior college instead of Virginia Beach. I would do anything to get a player, so I drove back to Virginia Beach, dropped off the first player, then headed for Garrett County Community College in the easternmost corner of Maryland. That meant nine more hours of driving. As we headed out my prize recruit jumped in the back seat and went to sleep. So much for the idea of giving him a recruiting pitch. He slept the whole way. When we arrived at his college he grabbed his bag and headed to his apartment. No sign of gratitude. No "Would you like a drink?" or "How would you like to crash on my couch since it's 3 in the morning and you drove for 12 straight hours?" Needless to say, when I headed out I didn't care how good a player he was. My recommendation was he was better off somewhere else. And I wasn't referring to another school.

On the return trip it started to snow. Great! Just what I needed. During my 12-hour drive back I resorted to two surefire methods of staying awake. The first was sticking my hand out the window as long as I could until it became practically frostbitten, then placing it under my armpit for a nice shot of adrenaline. The second was smoking a cigar. I found that it's very hard to fall asleep when you feel nausea and that's how I felt smoking a cigar. I finally returned the vice president's car Monday morning. Or was it in the afternoon? I wasn't quite sure. I know it was the last time he allowed anyone from the basketball coaching staff to borrow his car.

My sole disappointment about ACC was not getting the chance to coach the players I brought in because a month into the school year I landed a job as an assistant coach at Loyola College in Baltimore. It's funny how things work out and change your life forever.

Two weeks before getting the job at Loyola, I was turned down for the same position at the University of North Carolina-Wilmington. After losing out at UNC-Wilmington I went back to ACC to drown my sorrows with my officemate. I woke up the next morning with beer cans strewn all over my office and a massive hangover. In the end it was a lucky break because the UNC-Wilmington head coach was fired the following season. I would have been looking for another job instead of setting the course for my first head coaching position and meeting my future wife.

Before leaving for Loyola, I had to tell the players. For the first time in my coaching career I realized the type of impact I had on young people. As I spoke to the players I noticed that some of them were upset, especially Ricky Melendez, the guy from my hometown. It took me a long time to convince him to stay and understand that Coach Edwards would stand by him.

Jauss, the baseball coach, planned a going-away party for that night. As the evening wound down, someone started a bonfire by the baseball field. Before we knew it everyone was laughing and singing. It was one of the best moments of my life, seeing those guys from different backgrounds coming together. It was no wonder ACC went on to win 50 games the next two years and in each season reached the NAIA national tournament. Before my arrival at ACC, the Bulldogs had only one winning season in 17 years.

CHAPTER FIVE

Charm City or Charmed Life

Moving to Loyola College was a no-brainer. I was a full-time assistant at a NCAA Division I school working for a head coach on the rise (Mark Amatucci had been named the ECAC-Metro Coach of the Year the preceding season.) Plus, I almost doubled my salary again. I made $13,000 and didn't have to run the intramural program.

Working for Coach Amatucci greatly influenced how I coached in the years that followed. He was a man-to-man defense disciple who was in your face whether you were on the court or not. He genuinely cared for his players, even when he was screaming at the top of his lungs. At the end of the day you always knew he had your back.

The interview took place on a hot day in September 1985. School had already started when Amatucci's former assistant left for a job at Notre Dame. I drove up in my best suit, my only suit. A wool one to boot. By the time I reached Baltimore I had perspired through my shirt and pants. When we met at The Golden Arm, a joint owned by Johnny Unitas, Amatucci was dressed in a torn T-shirt and shorts with paint stains on them. When you're the boss you dress as you like. The suit worked for me and I landed the job.

Moving up to Division I at Loyola College in Baltimore.

Recruiting at Loyola took on a whole new meaning. As a Division I school, we were able to zero in on a player and work him as hard as we wanted. Back then you could see a player an unlimited number of times and talk to them on the phone every day. It gave the little guy an opportunity to outwork the big guy.

During my first week, Coach Amatucci joined me on my initial home recruiting visit to New Jersey. We went there to visit Marques Hamwright at the same time Hurricane Gloria pummeled the Jersey Shore. Undaunted, we pressed on. Once we made it to Hamwright's house he answered the door wearing a University of Delaware T-shirt. I made him change the shirt before Coach Amatucci saw it. When we finished our visit, I drove back through one of the worst storms of my life. But he came to Loyola, so the trip was worth it.

Two players from Baltimore I recruited with the most zeal were Thomas Jordan and Kevin Green. The former went to Oklahoma State while the latter became the all-time leading scorer at Loyola College.

Jordan was raised by his grandmother. We got to know each other very well, and we split a tuna salad sandwich for lunch every time he came to campus for a workout. In the end, his desire to go away and a lure of the perks that go with a Big 12 school won him over. I guess I should have given him the whole sandwich. At least once.

Green was a shy kid who was the first student (not just a basketball player) from Dunbar High School to attend Loyola. I'm convinced my effort led to his decision because I saw him 41 straight days. In January and February I saw him at every practice and every game. In the end, I really believe that's what sold him. Either that or the fact I bought enough candy from the cheerleaders each day to buy a whole new set of uniforms for them.

During my second year on staff at Loyola (1986-87), we signed seven new players. As the only full-time assistant I was also the recruiting coordinator. It was a remarkable year, not only for depth, but size as well. Four of the players were 6-foot-7 or bigger. Subsequently, *Eastern Basketball Magazine* ranked our recruiting class in the top 10 for eastern schools.

The recruit who stands out the most in my mind is Mike Wagner. He was a 6-foot-11 post player who made visits to West Virginia, Providence and Charlotte. Wagner grew up in a blue collar family from Beaver Falls, Pennsylvania. We hit it off immediately. During the fall recruiting period I flew to Pittsburgh every Monday and Wednesday to see him work out. Thanks to US Air I was able to make the round trip in one day. His parents were great people who had a genuine interest in finding the right place for their son and they were not blinded by the bright lights the bigger schools offered. In fact, during the home visit, Wagner's father served me a home-cooked meal that would have made my mother proud. I got fed and we got the kid. A great deal!

My biggest recruiting victory at Loyola was that of my future wife, Sandy Lanahan. She was the women's lacrosse head coach at the time. I'm very thankful she stooped to give a lowly assistant the time of day. Thinking I was safe a few years, I promised her we'd get married when I got my first head coaching job. As it turned out the timetable was moved up.

I ended up being Amatucci's top assistant for three years, but I almost lost my job on my first scouting trip. And if that had happened, I would have lost my chance to court Sandy.

Before the NCAA changed the rule about scouting opponents, coaches saw an opponent at least once in person depending on the travel distance. On my first scouting trip I was assigned to watch Hardin-Simmons University in Abilene, Texas. As I boarded the plane to Dallas, I had no idea what I was about to encounter.

Upon landing in Dallas I proceeded to the rental car agency. When I was asked for my credit card, I knew I was in trouble. You see, up to that point, I had never rented a car. Nor did I own a credit card. However, I did have about $500 in cash on me. After arguing with the agent, she told me the only way I could get a car without a credit card was by proving to her I intended to return to Baltimore. I also had to prove I was employed for more than a year at Loyola College. The first part was easy, but the second part was obviously a stretch. It was a Saturday afternoon. Nobody was in the office, so I did the only thing I thought of at the moment. I gave her the number to the priest's residence and told her to ask for Father Mac. He was our team chaplain. Father Mac traveled with us on road trips and would say mass for the players and coaches. How could I ask or expect him to lie for me? When she reached him, he told her that he knew me, but I had not been there a year. The agent denied me the car.

I was in a panic mode. I went to another rental car agency. Before I approached the new agency I placed a call to the good father explaining my situation. I told him if I didn't get to that game, I would be fired. I had to ask him to lie for me. Can you imagine asking a priest to lie? I went to a Catholic school for 12 years. If my mother had known, she would have disowned me. He said he couldn't do that, but he was willing to help. I had no choice but to take another swing.

As the next agent spoke with him, a smile came over her face. She allowed me to rent the car. I went to the game, but couldn't wait to get back to Baltimore to find out what he told her. When I asked him, Father Mac said he told her that coaches were hired and fired so often that he couldn't keep track. Thanks Father Mac for saving my job.

The next scouting trip wasn't any better. I drove to see a game at Long Island University in Brooklyn. I know it doesn't make sense, but that's where it is. I parked my car in a garage that closed at 11 that night. The game ran long, so by the time I returned to the garage, it was closed. I couldn't get my car out till the next morning. Fortunately for me, the assistant at Rutgers did the same thing. We shared a cab back to his place, then he brought me back the next morning. I had exactly four hours to get from Brooklyn to Baltimore and catch the team flight for California. Without traffic the drive takes about four-and-a-half hours. Thank goodness the police didn't catch me on that drive. I would have lost my license for sure. I was already on probation for previous speeding tickets. In fact, when I arrived at Loyola, the head coach had to write the judge in North Carolina on my behalf to tell him I needed my license to be hired. Another stipulation was that I would not drive in North Carolina for a year.

As my mother always told me things happen in threes. So it was no surprise that my third scouting trip was as much an adventure as the first two. I was assigned to scout Santa Clara, so naturally I flew out to see them in person. No problem with the rental car or parking, but something happened to me physically that I will never forget.

Sandy and I flew out the night before the game. I thought since I hadn't been able to spend much time with her that this would be a great opportunity. We arrived in San Francisco after 9 and went out to eat. That's where my trouble started. Later that night I felt sick to my stomach and the next morning I felt even worse. As I went into the Toso Pavillion

I felt the need to go to the bathroom (or should I say run) and get what was left in my stomach out of me.

While in the stall I heard my former althetics director, Tom O'Connor (then the AD at Santa Clara and later the 2008 head of the NCAA tournament selection committee) talking outside the door. Not wanting to make a bad impression I was as quiet as one could be while losing my cookies in the toilet. When I walked out I was white as a ghost, but still managed a quick hello before going into the arena. Scouting the game took a tremendous amount of will power and a lot of Sprite to get me through it. To this day I don't think Mr. O'Connor realized how sick I was. Flying back to Baltimore that night, Sandy had memories of San Francisco and the Winchester House while I had nightmares about the bathroom in Toso Pavillion. Must have been the soup!

In my last summer at Loyola I planned to run a basketball camp in New York with Bob Valvano, who was then the head coach at St. Francis College in Brooklyn. That camp opened the door for my first head coaching position. In preparation for the camp I met Carlo Tramontozzi, the St. Francis College athletics director. When Valvano accepted a professional coaching position overseas, I was perfectly positioned to be his successor at St. Francis.

My interview phase for the head coaching position at St. Francis was yet another unique interview experience. The common denominator was the setting. For Atlantic Christian, an airport; for Loyola, a bar. My interview with Tramontozzi took place at his favorite Italian deli in Brooklyn. First we met in his office, then walked down the street to a place called Nino's.

He explained the job's parameters in very simple terms, "I want you to win, I want you to graduate your players, but most important, you will be fired if you ever go over budget." He also told me I had five years to get it done. Win and you move. Lose and you move. That's how he summed it up. In his final remarks, he emphasized he would always back me as long as I didn't get him in trouble. If only more athletics directors took his approach. Of all the ADs for whom I worked, Tramontozzi was by far the most candid.

Our interview was cut short when his wife called to tell him new furniture had arrived, but the deliverymen would not move the furniture upstairs. So off we went to move the furniture. To this day I'm not sure if he hired me because he thought I was a good coach or because I moved his new couch without nicking the wall.

In July 1988, I was hired as the head coach of the St. Francis Terriers. At 27, I became the youngest head coach in Division I college basketball at the time for a whopping payday of $31,000 a year. Sounds like a big deal, but the truth is it was a job nobody wanted. Rumor had it two high school coaches were offered the job, but turned it down because they didn't want to take a pay cut. I didn't care. That was going to be my UCLA. I believe a few years earlier Lefty Driesell used the same line when he took the Maryland job. I guess neither one of us was right.

Though I moved down only one chair on the bench, I soon found out there is a big difference between making suggestions and making decisions. I felt I was ready. I was 2-0 as an assistant because, in one instance each at Atlantic Christian and Loyola, the head coach was thrown out during a game. At Loyola we came back to win on the road at Robert Morris in Pittsburgh. At ACC we lost by two points fewer than when the head coach was tossed. I'm the only one who thinks that counts as a win.

July is normally a heavy recruiting time in college basketball, but that summer for me was a time to meet my new players and find myself a place to live. Since St. Francis is primarily a commuter school, the only housing options for players were at home or an apartment close to campus. Since we recruited them, the responsibility fell upon the coach to find them a place. So I was on the lookout for myself and the players. I'm pretty sure Roy Williams didn't get his start at North Carolina looking for new digs for his players.

Meeting the new players was easier because my best two players were in that pick-up game I played in to recruit Ricky Henry. His brother, Rodney, and their buddy, Darwin Purdie, were already enrolled at St. Francis. Together they became the Terriers all-time leaders in assists and scoring. I promised

The youngest head coach in Division I at age 27. I kept the mustache to make me look older.

the players that when they got to school in the fall they'd have nice apartments.

Finding a place to live for Sandy and me was the easy part. We moved into the duplex Valvano owned. We rented it while he and his wife lived in Sweden. A win-win for both of us. As I promised Sandy, we became engaged with a date to be wed the following March. I checked my recruiting calendar and found that the weekend of March 11, 1989, no games were scheduled. Our nuptials were set for then, but our honeymoon had to wait until August (a non-recruiting month).

Another perk for moving into Valvano's house was his mother's cooking. Every month, when I went by his mother's house to drop off the rent check, she invited me in to eat and visit. She was your stereotypical

Italian mother who felt the need to feed any visitor. I really enjoyed those visits while learning about her husband, Rocco, also a former coach. And her cooking was phenomenal! On one occasion she invited me to a family meal at a restaurant, then refused to let me pay. I will always have a soft spot in my heart for her and the way she treated me like family.

There was one minor drawback to living in the Valvano duplex. It was located in Uniondale, which would have been very convenient if I had the head job at Hofstra University. St. Francis, on the other hand, was more than an hour away. But looking back, the friendship I developed with Mama Valvano was worth the increased travel time to work.

During the first couple weeks on the job, I stayed at my athletics director's brownstone while he visited family members in Italy. It was convenient and free. The first day I parked my car a couple blocks from the school. Parking in New York is always an adventure. I had two choices: Park in a garage and pay what seemed like a down payment on an apartment or take a chance on the street. And I mean a huge chance. If left on the street too long, it would be towed or broken into. The first day I decided to take a chance.

As I left my office that day I weighed my options. Should I try to find a closer spot to the brownstone or leave it where it was for the night? It was about midnight, so I didn't feel like looking for another space. By choice I walked back to the brownstone.

The next morning, as I approached the car to move it, I saw the driver's side

St. Francis College: One city block and seven stories high.

door was slightly open. "I don't remember leaving it open," I thought. Someone apparently saw my Maryland license plates and decided it was the perfect car to rob. Besides taking my car radio, everything inside was taken. Well, almost everything. I can only imagine the look on the thief's face when popping open the trunk and finding four garment bags of suits and three gym bags with all the clothes I owned. Inside one of the gym bags was the engagement ring I had planned to give my fiancée that weekend. The only items left behind were two tennis rackets. Even my golf clubs were taken, so I guess the thief played golf, not tennis.

Over the course of my three years in New York, my car was stolen three times. Not exactly material for a Chamber of Commerce brochure in the Big Apple. Two of the cars I got back and one was left in East New York. In the first instance, I received a call from a taxi driver who informed me it was parked in front of his apartment building. He said I could either call the police or he would pick me up. If the police impounded the car, it would cost me $125 to get it back. If he took me to it, it would cost me cab fare. I chose the cab fare. I drove my car to the police station and told them I recovered it. When I told the officer on duty it was parked in the lot, he told me I could have been arrested for filing a false police report had I been stopped on my way back to the precinct. To save $125, it was worth the risk. I doubt a manhunt was underway to recover a beaten up 1980 Toyota Corolla.

My problems were not limited to car theft. In those same three years, I accumulated close to $10,000 in unpaid parking tickets (I lost count of the amount I actually paid). Fortunately, by the time we registered the cars in New York it was March, so we registered them in Sandy's name. That way if I ever move back I won't have to worry about my car getting impounded for being a scofflaw.

In August 1988, we moved into Valvano's house on Long Island. Living in New York had its pros and cons. Getting around was somewhat of a challenge. I was used to being minutes away from the school at which I worked. Now I was an hour and change away by car or train.

Taking the Long Island Railroad to the subway was a new experience for me. The only trains I saw growing up in Ohio were freight trains. The only time I saw a subway train was when I watched *Welcome Back Kotter* on television.

I'll never forget that first day. It should have been a snap. Catch the train from Freeport to Jamaica, transfer at Jamaica, then on to Penn Station for the switch to the subway. It started off on a bad note when I missed my connection in Jamaica. When I finally got to the subway I jumped on the wrong train and ended up in the Bronx. Not the greatest section of the Bronx either with run-down buildings and with the corners anchored by panhandlers and drug dealers. I jumped on the next train going in the opposite direction. By the time I arrived at the campus in Brooklyn Heights stop it was past noon.

Finding places for my players was not easy either. Brooklyn Heights, an area made famous by *The Patty Duke Show*, was only one subway stop from Wall Street and an area taken over by yuppies (young urban professionals). That meant the average two-bedroom apartment rented for $1,200 a month, a little above our price range since the players received a stipend of only $800 a month to cover food and rent. Another catch: The lease covered 12 months, but the players received a stipend for only nine. So there I was getting my start as a head coach and feeling more like a real estate agent. After spending nearly a month searching, I found four places that housed three players each and cost them only $400 apiece. Not bad. As anticipated, the leases covered 12 months, but I worried about that later.

By the end of my Terriers coaching tenure I had quite a few landlords wanting my scalp. It wasn't as if I cheated them though. Every time a lease was broken the landlords kept the deposit. I thought that was fair compensation. Through those years players lived in a hotel, above a bar and a Mexican restaurant and neighboring a future rap group by the name of Guy. They became our most famous and biggest fans.

Once I found apartments I had to find beds. My assistants and I found the best deals at the Salvation Army. I could outfit each apartment for less than $100. Years later I did the same thing for my players at UMKC. The only difference was in Kansas City it was at a Goodwill Store, which cost a bit more than $100.

Two incidents occurred in my last year at St. Francis that convinced me I was not going to be a real estate agent anymore. First, in the middle of the season when checking on a couple of players, I found out the landlord didn't turn on the heat. But the topper was when one of the guys pointed to a hole in the wall where he said a rat the size of a cat came out. At that point I was not going to stick around. We were moving. I called my assistant and we moved the players to a new place in the middle of the night.

The second incident unfolded when we found a beautiful new place and the rent was extremely low. A couple of weeks before moving in, my assistant drove by the place, called me at midnight and told me to come by the new apartment. When I arrived I noticed a couple of hookers on the porch doing business. Now I understood why it was so cheap. That block turned into party central at night. I know I told the players that if they came to New York they would have a good time, but that's not what I had in mind. Cross that place off the list.

My first staff was easy to assemble. I looked for volunteers. My budget included $5,000 for assistants' salaries and I spent it all to keep

Joe Maniaci from the previous staff. An experienced high school teacher in Long Island, he proved to be the constant voice of reason. He drove in every day from Long Island and I'm sure he lost money when you subtract what he paid for gasoline.

I planned to have as my two volunteers a holdover from the previous staff, Tom Keenan and a first-year coach by the name of Ted Lewis. After the first couple weeks Keenan stopped coming by the school. Finally when I called his house, he answered and told me he would be by on Monday. That day came and went and I never heard from him again. He vanished into thin air. It became a running joke that I was still so sure that Keenan was going to come by on Monday. I just didn't know which Monday.

It should be noted that Lewis, a young buck full of energy, joined my staff based on the recommendation of a friend, Larry Shyatt. He was an assistant at the University of New Mexico where Ted had been a manager. Based on his reference I took a chance. After all, it didn't cost me anything. Ted was the son of Al Lewis, better known as Grandpa on *The Munsters*. In addition to being an actor, Al Lewis was a self-proclaimed talent scout. The first time he came to one of our games he told me how he discovered Lew Alcindor (Kareem Abdul-Jabbar). I looked at him and thought two things, "They didn't spend any money on makeup for him," and "How hard was it to tell that Alcindor was going to be a player?" Let's be honest. My mother could have seen Alcindor and known he was going to be a great player.

Maniaci and Lewis were the perfect assistants for me that year. On one hand Maniaci provided a sense of balance and kept me on an even keel. Lewis was a go-getter moving a mile a minute. We had some interesting times together that first year. I owe them more than they can imagine.

Before the season started, I came to grips with some of the quirks of St. Francis. The school was basically one building that filled an entire city block. My only way in was through a set of doors past a security booth. That was fine during the week, but on the weekends I needed to be on the guard's list to enter the building. I found out early there were no exceptions. Even Tramontozzi, my boss, had trouble before I got there. Doubling as the soccer coach and en route to the NCAA soccer tournament, he went to pick up the uniforms on a Saturday morning. But one of the guards wouldn't let him by since he wasn't on the list. Tramontozzi became so frustrated he threw a garbage can through a window and went in another way. Knowing that, I made sure I was always on the list.

The same guards controlled the lights in the gym. That meant we could only get in there at regularly scheduled times. In my mind that wouldn't work because I wanted my players to come in whenever they wanted. But the guards were the only ones with a key to the light switch and they guarded it like gold.

To counter that, one of my assistants and I devised a plan that resembled *Mission: Impossible*.

It took me a month before I got one of the guards to lend me the key to turn on the lights. When that happened "the mission" was on. I quickly tossed it to my assistant who sprinted out the back door. The alarm went off and I occupied the guards long enough for my assistant to make a copy at the hardware store. The guards never realized he set off the alarm. Problem solved.

Another early challenge was pre-season conditioning. Since we only used the gym for practice times, I didn't want to waste time running sprints. The first option was running outside. I decided that was too dangerous when my center almost got hit by a cab while running across the Brooklyn Bridge. From that point on we ran on the roof of the school. That worked as long as we didn't hit the soft spots up there and the wind didn't blow too hard.

The team I inherited had a legitimate chance of recording a winning record for its first time in close to two decades. They came close the year before, but a late-season collapse prevented a winning ledger. I had a solid core made up of a good group of seniors. It was a matter of how quickly they would adjust to a new coach.

My second day on the job, the Terriers sports information director left. I quickly found out when someone departs St. Francis they're not quickly replaced. Something about the budget or the vow of poverty Catholic priests take. So there I was putting together my first media guide. It wasn't going to win any awards, but it was a pretty solid recruiting tool.

I was also the equipment manager. At most schools they hire someone to take care of the equipment and wash clothes after practice. The person to do that at St. Francis was me. To my players from that first year, I apologize for using too much bleach and fabric softener.

One thought on opening practice. Or Midnight Madness that is. Since we had Midnight Madness each year at Loyola, I decided to carry it on at St. Francis. Places like Kentucky and North Carolina draw thousands of fans for that event. As midnight approached our place was empty. We ended up starting our first practice in front of three bums who came in from the cold. Didn't matter to me. We still toasted with champagne and cut down the nets.

We opened the 1988-89 season at home against Winthrop University of Rock Hill, South Carolina. It was a close contest all the way, and the Terriers held on for a 58-56 win. After the game my assistants and I took the train over to Chinatown and celebrated the victory with

a table full of food. Then we walked over to Little Italy for some dessert.
As we walked down the street, I felt a long way from a steel mill town
outside Cleveland. I started to hum the Frank Sinatra tune *My Way*. I
thought if I could make it at St. Francis I could make it anywhere. Why
not? I was undefeated as a head coach and on my way.

Getting my point across to Lester James (#42).

On the train ride home that
night, I felt on top of the world.
When I reached the station at
Jamaica I was absolutely jacked
with emotion. As I waited for the
next train I noticed a guy with a St.
Francis College jacket on. Feeling
compelled to approach him I
introduced myself and invited him
to our next game. We drew only
a couple hundred fans per game,
so I thought we could always use
another fan. As he turned around
I noticed he had only one eye.
Not that it was hard to notice. In
the other eye area was an empty
socket. He didn't try to hide the
empty socket with a patch or
glasses or anything. I recoiled a little, then I thought, "If we play poorly
he only has to cover one eye." There I was at the train station talking
to a guy who most likely picked up the St. Francis jacket off the street,
but, hell, I invited him to our next game anyway. New York has a way of
keeping a person humble.

The following Wednesday I attended the weekly New York Area Metropolitan Basketball Writers Association luncheon. As I entered Madison Square Garden, where the luncheon took place, I spotted St. John's University coach, Lou Carnesecca. I walked over to introduce myself. As I extended a handshake, he grabbed my cheek, squeezed it and with a big grin on his face said, "Welcome to New York, Richie!" Imagine my surprise. I was shocked he knew who I was, but even more astounded to be treated like a long lost son. During my time in New York I was able to see why so many adore Coach Louie. He was a masterful tactician and an even better person.

At the luncheon each coach in the New York metro area normally stood up, reviewed his team's progress and previewed the upcoming games. At 1-0, I was ready to go. The only problem was most of the writers were too busy eating and talking among themselves instead of listening to the low major coaches. I was more than a little disappointed in their response to my good news about the Terriers. However, when P.J. Carlesimo, the head coach at Seton Hall at the time, rose to speak they quieted down and picked up their pads and pens. The first words out of his mouth were music to my ears. He ripped them for not showing the proper respect to all of the coaches in the room. He was the former coach at Wagner College, so I was impressed with the fact that he didn't forget about his coaching roots. Now in the NBA, Carlesimo still hasn't changed.

In coaching, you find out you're only as good as your next game. Our next contest was against Wagner, under Carlesimo's successor, Neil Kennett. We took the bus over to Staten Island loaded with confidence. Clinging to a one-point lead we inbounded the ball to Juan Jorge, a good free throw shooter. With a man open on the other end of the floor, instead of throwing it down and letting the final seconds run out, he held the ball and took the foul. "Shooting a one-and-one, leading by one on the road is okay," I thought to myself. Kennett called a timeout to freeze the shooter. In the huddle I emphasized getting back on defense in case Jorge missed. In so doing, I committed a cardinal sin in basketball. I knew it as soon as the words left my lips, but I couldn't get them back. I "black cowed" the shooter. In other words, I put a negative thought in his mind. Well, he missed and Wagner scored in transition to pull out a one-point victory, which sent me to my first loss as a head coach. There went my undefeated season.

A few years later I realized every season turns on two or three games or incidents that will either make or break a team. I recall a couple, one of which occurred the year before I was hired at St. Francis.

During the previous school year the athletic department did not meet the minimum number of sports required by the NCAA, so St. Francis was not eligible for the Northeast Conference tournament. An appeal hung over our heads throughout my first season, giving us some hope. It also meant the tournaments we played in during the season took on a more significant meaning. Knowing that before the season started, I tried to use it to my advantage.

The first tournament we played in was at Dartmouth in New Hampshire. At every tournament each player would customarily receive a gift, anything from a bag to a Sony Walkman. My guys hoped for the Walkman. Instead each received a beautiful Cross pen. You should have seen the look on their faces. I still have eight or nine of those pens.

In that tournament the Terriers split the two games while averaging 92 points. We put the ball in the basket, but didn't do much on the other end. The split, which moved the Terriers to 5-3 on the year, gave us some momentum heading into what became the trip from hell.

Valvano, as my predecessor, set up a trip to the West Coast to play San Diego State and U.S. International. To play games out of the region meant covering our travel costs with guarantees, i.e. money the home team paid for you to compete in its arena. There was no obligation for the home team to play a return game in New York. To pay for the trip, the Terriers played Southern Utah University on the way back to New York. On paper it looked like the ideal trip. Previously the Terriers beat U.S. International on a neutral court, and SUU was in its first year of competing as a Division I school. Then after a day at home, the schedule called for us to fly to Canada for a tournament in Nova Scotia. The dynamics changed when the tournament director moved it up a day, thus wiping out our trip home. Instead of resting, we traveled for more than 24 hours.

We flew to San Diego on Christmas. That was our chance to bond as a team. Some time on the road together away from all the distractions was beneficial. At least that was my plan. Since we had an extra day before our first game we took the team to the world famous San Diego Zoo. Since many of them had never been to a zoo, it was a great educational experience for them. I enjoyed watching the kangaroos.

Unfortunately, the next day the Terriers played like they were still at the zoo. San Diego State beat us pretty badly, then U.S. International avenged its previous loss to us. That meant spending New Year's Eve in San Diego after back-to-back losses. I never took losses well and that was no exception. After watching the tape of the U.S. International game, I decided to drown my sorrows with a few beers.

The next morning my fiancée, who made that trip, looked forward to some whale watching and sightseeing in San Diego. As I proceeded down the gang plank toward the boat, all I thought was, "I should be back with my team trying to figure out how to beat Southern Utah."

Those thoughts quickly slipped out of my head the moment the boat left the dock. I spent the next two hours draped over the side of the boat losing my lunch in the Pacific Ocean. Sandy was as happy with my performance as I had been the previous night with my team. It was the last basketball trip she ever made.

Southern Utah proved to be more of an adventure than I bargained for. To get to its campus in Cedar City, we flew to Las Vegas and made a three-hour bus ride. That was a trip I later became very familiar with at UMKC, since we were Mid-Continent Conference foes for my seven years there. No doubt my first impression was the most memorable.

They were very good and well-coached. I love when coaches use that phrase. When used after a game it's definitely "coach speak." Translation: They kicked our tails. Saying it before a game typically means the coach doesn't really know a lot about the opponent and doesn't want to say anything to motivate the other team. If a coach makes that statement and he's familiar with the opponent, however, it means the players follow the coach's directions very well. In this case it was the former, not the latter.

From the outset, I could tell it was going to be a long night. Then, with about 11 minutes to go in the game and the score already out of hand, I lost my composure. While protesting a call my shoe flew onto the floor. As I walked toward the half court area to retrieve it, there was a possession change and the trailing official turned to run toward the other end. At that moment, I froze. As we collided, I thought I had position and he would call a charge on himself. Instead, looking at me with my shoe in my hand, he tossed me out of the game. Twelve games into my career, I was ejected from my first game because my shoe came off my foot. At least that's how I choose to remember it. Little did I know it was only one act in the aforementioned road trip from hell.

After the game, we piled into the bus and headed for Vegas. While waiting at the airport for our red-eye back to New York, I mindlessly popped a couple quarters in the slot machine. While sitting there trying to figure out how to get the momentum back, my team captains (Rodney Henry and Darwin Purdie) approached me. I was down, but my players expressed their confidence about the upcoming conference games. Rodney Henry is one of the greatest young men I had the privilege of coaching. He showed me the true meaning of leadership that day. I was very lucky to have such a great captain in my first year as a head coach.

It was 4 in the afternoon when we landed in New York and our flight to Toronto departed four hours later. As we walked over to the terminal for international departures, there was a new spring in my step. We landed in Toronto at 9:30 that night, then caught another flight to Halifax. We thought we'd be in bed shortly before midnight. At least that was the plan.

Our flight to Toronto was delayed, so we missed our connection. As a result, we boarded a cargo plane. Sounds like *Planes, Trains and Automobiles*, doesn't it? If you've never been on a cargo plane, I would not recommend it. All the supplies are in the front and the passengers are jammed behind an erected wall in the back.

Three hours behind schedule, we were informed it was going to be a rough ride into Halifax due to a heavy snowstorm. Rough was an understatement. By the time we touched down there was not an empty airsickness bag on the plane. It was 4 in the morning when we arrived at the hotel. Not only did we travel for more than 24 hours but through at least five time zones. I lost count. My only hope was that our opponent in the first round would be really mediocre.

The first night we played as well as we played before our trip to the West Coast. Purdie was unstoppable and we won comfortably. The next night was an exhibition game against a Canadian national team, not part of the tournament. That was the night that changed our season.

Before the game Purdie, the team's best player, asked me how much he was going to play and whether or not he should get taped. I told him only a few minutes, but advised him to get taped anyway. Kids are kids and sometimes they don't listen. Four minutes, 53 seconds into the game, Purdie went down with a sprained ankle. Funny how you always remember the time and score of a crucial event in a basketball game. As the trainer brought him over to the bench I could tell he wasn't taped. He missed the next ten games. On the positive side, with the other players picking up the slack, we ended up winning the tournament. It was the Terriers first in-season tournament championship since the 1950s.

We opened up conference play losing our first eight games. Then Purdie came back and we won five of our last seven. The winning season we dreamed about took a serious blow on that trip north of the border. In my first year as head coach we ended up 14-16. At UCLA or North Carolina that type of season would be looked upon as a complete failure, but at St. Francis it was the second highest win total in 20 years.

One conference game stands out in particular. It was against Loyola College and my boss, Mark Amatucci. It would be the first time I had went up against someone I had previously worked for. As fate would have it there were also some burning issues from the previous season.

During the last game between the two teams, Mike Morrison had been the recipient of a hard foul going in for a layup. The player who committed the foul was John Flannigan. Mike's father thought the foul was intentional and meant to do harm. He was so incensed that he came out of the stands and attacked John. It took a few minutes for security to regain control of the situation. Mr. Morrison was rejected and Flannigan's jersey was ripped. Both players were still playing for their respective teams, but thankfully, Mr. Morrison did not attend the game.

The game was a tight one and it looked like we were going to pull out our first conference win after Steve Mickens sank a 15-foot jump shot to put us up by one point. However, on the next possession Morrison hit the game winner and we were denied. I was happy for Mike, but would have been happier if he had missed the shot.

Also, I learned some valuable coaching lessons on managing players. Treating everyone fairly was the most important thing, but that didn't mean you treated them all the same. I always loved all my players, but that doesn't mean I'd want all of them to marry my daughter.

For example, as we were coming off the court early in the season, I grabbed Purdie and screamed at him about a mistake he made at the end of the half. He was so distraught he punched a hole in a fire door that led to the weight room. (The metal door was about a foot thick.). Once inside he picked up a Universal machine and shoved it across the floor. To give you an idea how much the machine weighed, it took eight guys to push it back in place. After witnessing that I noted, "Never yell at Purdie during the game."

Another odd wrinkle to our airline travel was our traveling party. For our radio broadcaster, Todd Ant, to fly, I had to find the money. The school allowed us only enough money to purchase plane tickets for our players, coaches and trainer. That meant I had to either hope for an injury or suspend a player. Bad luck or fortuitous luck, Ant made every trip in my three years there. The first year was due to a player suspension, the second because of a season-ending injury to a reserve and the third year because a player quit the team.

My second season brought a tremendous amount of change on and off the court. Sandy was pregnant with Colin, our first child. We moved into a three-family house in the Bay Ridge area of Brooklyn, which was closer to the school. The rent was a little on the steep side, but it was the house of Tony Manero, the John Travolta character in the movie *Saturday Night Fever*. Every so often I'd wake up in the middle of the night with the urge to dance.

On the court, four seniors graduated and I lost my coaching staff. However, the Terriers AD rewarded my first season with additional funding. That meant, for the first time in school history, the program was budgeted for a full-time assistant coach. Immediately I hired Chris Casey and Glen Braica. Both were young guys who had a great feel for the situation. Today they are doing well on the staff at St. John's in nearby Jamaica.

Recruiting took on a whole new method at St. Francis. We didn't have the budget even for gas, so instead of driving throughout the country we used the money for subway tokens. The only times I recruited outside New York were either because of a tie to an area through a coach or to see a junior college regional tournament. A tournament gave me the ability to see more prospects at once and an opportunity to target East Coast players who might want to come home.

Campus visits were based on selling New York on a subway. Our pitch was "The Big Apple could be yours for a dollar." Every visit included a trip to the Brooklyn Sports Page Saloon. It was the original sports bar in the area. As a coach you try to choreograph every second of a campus visit, but with our first recruit, Tracy Turner, it didn't go exactly as planned. After the tour of the Brooklyn Promenade, where some scenes from the movie *Moonstruck* were filmed, we walked over to the Brooklyn Sports Page Saloon for dinner. When the waiter came over, I ordered an iced tea. Turner and his player host, Steve Mickens, at the table followed suit. When the waiter brought the iced teas I knew something was wrong. Tracy at the end of the table smiled from ear to ear. So did Steve. When I sipped it, I realized it was a Long Island Ice Tea. Tracy probably thought that I was a really cool coach. Though I sent the drinks back, Tracy still signed with St. Francis.

We had what I felt was a good recruiting class. We signed three high school players that made college all-freshmen teams. Unfortunately, only one of them ended up playing at St. Francis. Our first signee was a shooter out of Cincinnati by the name of Aaron Nichols. The other two players were Darrick Suber out of Pittsburgh and Lou Myers from Philadelphia. All three signed an institutional letter of intent and sent them to us.

Unlike most schools, St. Francis did not participate in the National Letter of Intent program because the school did not want to pay the extra money. The NLI program was started by the old Southwest Conference to ensure football players did not change their minds once they committed to a school. The program is not governed by the NCAA; therefore, schools can choose whether to participate in the program.

An institutional letter of intent combined with financial aid was the only binding document at St. Francis. However, it only bound the school to the student and not the other way around. Not being part of the NLI program hurt us initially, but eventually it helped me land one of the best players ever to play at St. Francis.

A week after Nichols signed, he called to tell me his father wanted him to visit The Citadel. He assured me he wasn't interested in a military college. He was only making the trip out of respect for his father. What could I say? He was not legally bound to come to St. Francis. After his visit he told me he was going to The Citadel, then tried to tell me how it wasn't really like the military. I asked if he had to wear a uniform, march and attend roll call every morning. The answer was yes to all three questions.

Nichols lasted one year in which he made the all-freshmen team in the Southern Conference, then was dismissed for sneaking off-campus to a Burger King. Later he became a two-year starter for me at the University of North Florida.

Unlike Nichols, Suber arrived on campus and enrolled in classes. After three days he came into my office to tell me he wanted a school with more of a campus, so he was going home. Funny, it was the same campus he visited before enrollment. A couple of days later I called his house and reached his sister who spilled the beans. Rather than going home, as I was told, he took the bus to Rider University in Lawrenceville, New Jersey. Seems the coaching staff there talked to him the whole time he was on the St. Francis campus. In the end, convinced to leave, Suber went on to become one of the best players in Rider basketball history. I was really pissed off when I found out what happened. I knew Rider had his high school teammate on its roster, but I felt like I had won the recruiting war when Suber arrived and enrolled in classes. When I checked on whether he attended classes, I was told he didn't. Had he attended a class, Suber would have triggered his clock and lost a year of eligibility. Rider advised him well. At the time I didn't have the resources to make a big stink out of it. And if they used his high school teammate as a liaison, then it's not against NCAA rules. Unethical yes, illegal no. The only satisfaction I got was screaming at Rider's assistant coach on the phone.

The third player, Lou Myers, played for us and was selected to the Northeast Conference All-Freshmen team. Who knows how good we could have been with all three in a Terrier uniform?

Two other recruiting trips etched in my mind forever resulted from near-death experiences, one by snow and the other by gunfire. While the big-time coaches flew private planes into the junior college regional at Scottsbluff, Nebraska, I could only afford to fly into Denver. Free from rental car problems on that trip, I drove north to Cheyenne, Wyoming, then east to Scottsbluff. On a normal day that's about a four-hour drive. That day it took a whole lot longer. The snow started when I landed in Denver. By the time I reached Cheyenne it had become a full-blown blizzard. I kept pushing on for a couple of reasons. First, I had to get to the tournament. Second, I couldn't see the exit ramp. I was afraid if I got off the highway I might slide off the road and freeze to death in my car.

After nine hours on the road, I finally reached Scottsbluff. When I pulled into the gas station, the attendant asked me how I got through the gates. "What gates?" I asked. I found out the gates on the highway are closed when a blizzard hits. Whew! I was lucky I kept driving since no one was behind me. It took a couple of Irish hot chocolates to help calm my nerves from that episode.

The other recruiting destination was easier to reach, more difficult to depart. Since my early coaching days at Atlantic Christian I often went to see Jackie Knowles at the Webster (N.Y.) Police Athletic League Gym. You never knew whom you might find. One night while watching Lester James play, a drive-by shooting occurred. As the gunfire exploded through the windows, everyone in the gym dove for cover. I threw myself under the bleachers and stayed there long after the gunfire stopped. Fortunately, no one was hurt, so the games continued. I thought the place was supposed to be safe since it was the *Police* Athletic League.

With so many changes my second season with the Terriers was a long one, typified by a road game at Morgan State in Baltimore.

With its gym undergoing a renovation, the wall at one end was still under construction. The night St. Francis played there, the wind was blowing so hard we saw the net blowing in the wind when a player stepped to the foul line. Early in the second half, John Arnold, my point guard, was whistled for a foul. We had it as his third, but the official scorer had it as his fourth. My back-up point guard was injured, so the call was crucial. As I approached the scorer's table I saw the official scorer was a youthful looking girl. She appeared to me to be a high school student. After I argued my case for a couple of minutes, she shut the book and quit. The referee had no choice but to either get her back or call the game. At that point I should have told him to call the game. The rule states if the official scorer quits, the home team is liable and the visitor wins by forfeit. Five minutes later she was back and I was faced with a decision—go to my bench or face ejection. I should have taken the ejection. Two minutes later Arnold picked up his fifth, so our chances of winning slipped away. After the game we watched the tape and never found the mysterious third foul.

The only ray of hope that year was the transfer of three players from other schools who chose, as I envisioned, to move close to home. They had the ability to lift the program to the top of the league. Nerim Gjonbalaj (pronounced like Jon-bull-eye), Kent Bryant and Ron Arnold (John Arnold's cousin) were the foundation for the future. In addition we brought in five players to increase our recruiting class to eight. That was the overhaul I was looking for as I tried to establish the program.

Another job I had was director of promotions. There was no extra pay or title involved, but some unusual perks. When we were scheduled to play an exhibition game against the Irish national team, we didn't have the money to pay for their expenses, so we had to raise the funds. I solicited every Irish bar in the area to support us by participating in the

"Great Irish Shootout." For only $100 each bar sent its best shooter to see who could make the most three-point shots in a minute. Also, we had an Irishfest with live bands. We had more than enough money to cover expenses and, as a bonus, I took home all the unopened bottles of Harp beer. That was a good promotion!

One other bright spot that season was selling out our first two games. Though the listed capacity was only 2,000, a sellout is a sellout, the first since Jim Valvano brought his Iona team in ten years before. The line for tickets spilled out the front door and extended halfway around the block. When the fire marshall came in, it was a madhouse. The next day my athletics director told me we were discontinuing our relationship with the Brooklyn Sports Foundation, which left me dismayed since my relationship with them was the main reason for the sellout.

I felt like only at St. Francis would the school turn its back on a sellout because it created too much work. Later that spring the administration turned down Spike Lee and Michael Jordan when they wanted to use our gym for the first Nike commercials during the advertising campaign for Air Jordans. To accommodate them, the school would have been forced to move or cancel a couple physical education classes. But the administration decided the classes were more important than the free publicity and revenue the commercials would have generated.

That decision along with the administration's reluctance to allow me to run a summer camp opened my eyes to what they wanted from an athletic program. I busted my hump to put people in the seats for home games, but the school administration could not have cared less. For the first time I understood why few coaches lasted more than a couple years at St. Francis. Too often I felt like I was beating my head against the wall.

I keep thinking to this day, "Only at St. Francis would the administration turn its back on sure fire publicity bonanzas."

My third and what ended up to be my final season with the Terriers started with tremendous expectations. We had two or three potential all-conference players and the most depth in my three seasons there. We also had a group tied together by an emotional string. Point guard Lynn Smith had Big East ability, but with mood swings of someone with bipolar disorder. After graduation Smith was jailed after beating another player to death while playing in a men's league. When Smith's mind was right, his competitive fire made him one of my all-time favorites to coach.

Two of the three transfers were not eligible until the end of the first semester. So I set up the schedule so that they'd miss only the first four games. I believed they were worth the wait.

Nerim Gjonbalaj had gone to Akron University and was coached by Bob Huggins. In two exhibition games, Gjonbalaj paced the Zips in scoring. When Huggins found out he did not attend a single class, however, the coach sent him home. So much for the critics who say Huggins doesn't care about academics. Gjonbalaj returned to the Albanian section of Brooklyn where his mother promptly informed him that she would send him back to Albania if he didn't go back to college.

Gjonbalaj, a 6-foot-8 power forward, did things in the post you couldn't teach. He could have been one of the most dominant post players in the league, but he only played one game for us. In the opening game of the Terriers season, Gjonbalaj recorded a double-double with 18 points and 11 rebounds. He was unstoppable. On the bus ride home I envisioned, with Gjonbalaj manning the post, the Terriers cutting down the nets at the end of the year. Those visions were shattered the next day when he told me he intended to quit and follow his dream to be a tight end in professional football. He dreamed of following in the footsteps of former New York Giants tight end Mark Bavaro. I tried for a week to make him understand the Giants were not going to look at a college basketball player who quit his team. Besides, he hadn't even played high school football because his mother wouldn't let him. Now he's the head of security at Scores Gentleman's Club.

One transfer down, two to go. Kent Bryant transferred from Hofstra. I found out later in the year, when we played at Hofstra, that Bryant was banned from that campus as a result of an incident in the dorm. That was news to me; the coach at Hofstra didn't mention any issues when I called for a background check. When security tried to remove Bryant from the floor before our game there, I assured them he'd be departing with the team immediately after the game. It worked and they let him play. Bryant went on to be a solid role player, yet without the impact I envisioned.

The player who made an impact was Ron Arnold. A two-time all-city player at Rice High School, Arnold started out with the intention of playing for Coach Pete Gillen at Xavier University in Cincinnati. Unfortunately, as a Proposition 48 casualty, Arnold was ineligible to play in his first year because he did not meet academic eligibility standards. While sitting out, feeling alienated and alone in Ohio, he looked for a place closer to home. Two factors weighed in our favor. His cousin, John Arnold, was a sophomore on our team, and we were not bound by the letter of intent, which in that case helped us. It meant he wouldn't lose any eligibility if he transferred to St. Francis.

When John Arnold told me about Ron's desire to transfer I told him to call Ron, then I placed a call to Coach Gillen at Xavier. From our days of working camp I always considered him a friend, but in this instance he felt like I stabbed him in the back because he thought I tampered with Ron Arnold. I assured him I didn't make the initial contact. Ron Arnold called his cousin first. The reality was Arnold's AAU coaches shopped him around to schools in New York. Though we weren't on the AAU coach's list, I was only trying to be respectful of the situation. At the same time I felt he could be a stud for us, while at Xavier he would barely see playing time. There were two future NBA players there (Tyrone Hill and Derek Strong) who ate up most of the minutes. After the transfer, Ron Arnold definitely lived up to his reputation. He was voted the Northeast Conference Newcomer of the Year and became a three-time all-league player.

Recruiting is such a huge hype machine these days. One website after another quotes the so-called experts about the strengths and weaknesses of a player and his rank. If the average fan saw a picture and bio of those so-called experts, there might not be as much hype. Many of the people who run recruiting services never coached or played the game. Furthermore, very few have ever studied the game enough to understand what makes some players better than others. I found through the years that some of the players with less of a reputation coming in turn out to be a better player leaving. We found three of them in Lester James, Brian Jones, and Allen West. All three were very good players, yet quiet in the way they took care of business.

Lester was a 6-foot-7 forward from the Bronx who came to us from Jacksonville College, a juco in eastern Texas. He passed 23 hours in the spring of his sophomore year at Jacksonville, a huge class load considering the average schedule is only 15 hours. It showed what he was capable of when he put his mind to it, but he still came up one class short of graduation. That summer we suggested he enroll in a swim class at Bronx Community College. If he passed, our director of admissions, Brother George Larkin, would admit him into St. Francis. I don't know how to swim, so it was up to my assistant, Glen Braica, to help him get through the class. I wish I had pictures of Braica in the pool helping

Lester learn the breaststroke. Lester passed the class, became an all-league player and went on to play professionally in Europe.

Jones and West were the unsung heroes of the team. Both, while capably filling their roles, were instrumental in the team's success. West has since become a successful restaraunteur in Manhattan.

CHAPTER SIX

Someone Stole Our Uniforms

After losing our opener on the road and with our starting center (Gjonbalaj) off seeking fame and fortune in the NFL, we won our next four games in a row at home. Great scheduling! It was not easy to get home games, but through some hard work we were able to schedule more home games than road games. I took some lumps the previous year by starting two home-and-home series on the road. Also, I agreed to play Liberty home-and-home in the same year. Teams at the low major level of Division I do not have more home games in a season very often. Barely ever. Usually money from a road game helps supplement the entire athletic department budget. In other words, when the athletics director needs a little help in balancing the budget, the easiest way to make up the extra money is by sending a low major men's basketball team like the Terriers to play a game against a BCS school. Guarantee payments range from $50,000 to $100,000. It's a nice payday for the visitors, and the home team locks up another game for its season ticket package.

The Terriers started to play well at home, but struggled on the road before we finally had a breakthrough game. It was a seven-hour bus ride to Hamilton, N.Y., where we played against my old friend Jack Bruen and his Colgate team. The game was tight until one of the officials, Bob Barnett, called a forceout. That was a call in the NBA to prevent the officials from calling a foul on a superstar. There was only one problem with that call in college: It was never a rule. Either call a foul or out of bounds. When Jack heard the call he went absolutely ballistic. He took off his jacket and threw it at the official. Rightfully so, I might add. Of course I had no problem with the call because it was in my favor.

The official, Barnett, tossed him, and we went on to gain a much-needed win.

Perhaps Bruen's apparel problem foreshadowed a key to future successful road performances. Every year you read about a team changing the color of its uniforms for a special game to get motivation. That usually costs additional money, which we didn't have, but we still managed to make a color change, kind of.

Late in the season, we were scheduled to play a conference game at Monmouth University in New Jersey, and the team bus pulled up to its usual spot on the side of the school building (it couldn't fit out front). On that trip Braica loaded the uniforms into the travel bins on the side of the bus, then jumped on board. About five minutes later I came out to make sure everyone was on the bus and ready to go. They were. As I put my bag underneath I asked Braica if he brought out the uniforms. He said he did. I looked again and there was no bag. Someone had grabbed the uniform bag and slid down to the subway. It took a lot of chutzpah to do that in broad daylight with a bus loaded with passengers.

I had to call the head coach at Monmouth, Wayne Szoke, and ask permission to wear our team's home uniforms. Our only other option was to wear their road uniforms. He didn't want an intra squad game, so he relented. They wore their road uniforms, and we upset Monmouth on its senior night. My next call was to Liberty University's coach, Jeff Meyer, my counterpart for our next road game. Meyer kindly obliged and we won that game as well. Had I known better, I would have ditched our road uniforms earlier in the season.

The Northeast Conference tournament took place at the home of the higher seeds. That meant hosting Long Island University. I anticipated a great crowd because LIU was actually located two subway stops away in Brooklyn. In fact, that's how we traveled there. Recruiting is one thing, but I am positive I was the only Division I coach in America who turned in a receipt for subway tokens as a team travel expense. Talk about a cheap road game. Fifteen subway tokens covered all the expenses.

After winning the first round game I met with Dean Adams, the vice president of student affairs. Because it was an additional budget expense, I needed his approval to play in the semifinal game at St. Francis of Pennsylvania. He asked me if we could get out of playing the game to save the money. I told him I would take the money out of my pocket if I had to. Sensing my frustration, he relented and we were on our way to Loretto. While riding the bus I thought to myself, "Did Dean Smith ever have to worry about getting approval to travel to the ACC tournament?"

After solving the budgetary problem, we had another dilemma. Lou Myers, a starting guard for us was due in court—the court of law, that is—on the morning of the game. One of my assistants, Glen Braica, remained behind and brought him to the game once court adjourned. They arrived at game time. The game went back and forth until Mike Iuzzolino took over for the home team. He made three deep threes midway through the second half and we never recovered. It was a small consolation that he helped the "other" St. Francis to its first-ever NCAA tournament appearance and later played in the NBA for the Dallas Mavericks. In the locker room after the game I tried to console the team.

I also tried to make them understand we had everyone coming back. And had a great chance to win the league next year.

As if I weren't feeling bad enough, the bus broke down on the way home. The team had to be ferried to a rest area by the highway patrol. We sat for five hours in the rest area waiting for the bus to be fixed. With daylight fast approaching I told each one of my players how proud I was of his efforts and of the class displayed throughout the season. We transformed into a new team and managed to put together the Terriers' first winning season in almost two decades. For all of our success I was named the Northeast Conference Coach of the Year. Little did I know, sitting in the rest area, I had coached my last game at St. Francis College.

CHAPTER SEVEN

New York, Alaska or Florida

When the Terriers season ended I had the opportunity to interview for three different jobs. I was suddenly a hot commodity in the coaching world. First, I got a call from Richie Petrucinni, the athletics director at Iona College, which seemed like a great move. Higher profile, more resources and more money. They even had a house on campus for the head coach. That's where Jim Valvano made his mark before becoming the head coach at North Carolina State. On the day of my interview his younger brother, Bob, hooked me up with Jim on the phone so he could prepare me. After all, the athletics director had been Jim Valvano's team manager when he was at Iona. I stood outside the gym on a pay phone listening to Jimmy V as he told me everything I needed to know and what to say to get the job. It was no wonder the athletics director told a mutual friend I sounded a lot like a young Jim Valvano. In the end Iona went with an older, more experienced coach. So I was down to three options - the frozen tundra of Alaska, the sunny beaches of northern Florida or another year on the trains in Brooklyn.

Staying in Brooklyn would not have been such a bad thing. I liked my team, and we had enough talent to vie for the Northeast Conference championship. Also, I was very fond of all my players. They were a great group. Financially, however, it was killing me. My salary was still in the low $30K range, and without camp income I was treading water.

The other two options were unique opportunities. Alaska-Anchorage was a high-profile Division II school that hosts the Great Alaska Shootout every year. Cold on the outside, but hot in the gym. The athletics director told me Anchorage wasn't as cold as I thought. He told me it was due to the Japanese currents. All I know is there's snow on the ground ten months of the year. Who cares about Japanese winds or currents?

The University of North Florida was an opportunity to start a program from scratch at the NAIA level for one year, then move up to Division II before reaching its goal of becoming a Division I program. UNF had been classified as a NAIA school with its overall athletics program in existence only since 1983. Let's see, sun and surf? Or cold and snow?

The process at North Florida was very thorough to say the least. The athletics director, John Ratliff, wanted game tapes and phone numbers of a former player, booster and opposing coach, in addition to calls to all my references. Finally, Ratliff wanted each candidate to write a five-year plan encompassing all aspects of the Osprey (a bird) program. By the time I finished the plan, it was 21 pages. Then I met with three different committees over a two-day span. When it was over, I felt like I met half of Jacksonville. It was a cross between a proctology exam and an IRS audit.

With an offer in hand from the University of North Florida, I headed back to New York to negotiate a new contract at St. Francis College. I wasn't looking to break the bank. Truth is, there were only four things I wanted: 1. Since I was doing the job of an assistant athletics director, I wanted the title to go with it; 2. A multi-year contract (three years); 3.

Permission to run a basketball camp at the school (rent free for the first year); and 4. A parking place. The last request was the most valuable to me because I was tired of searching for a parking spot every morning. Worse yet, I was weary of three stolen cars. To his credit, my athletics director supported me fully, but the administration shot me down without any discussion at all. I was off to Florida.

To tie up loose ends, I informed the team I was leaving. That was hard, but calling my top recruit, Brian Sitter, was even more difficult because it was the second time in his career he signed with a school only to have the coach leave. That's the downside to the letter of intent. A player is bound to a school even if the coach leaves. The argument that a player chooses a school based only on the school is totally ridiculous, but you will never get an administrator to admit it. (My first thought was to have him attend UNF, but that meant clearing it with the UNF athletics director.)

Sometimes things are not what they appear to be, and that goes for people as well. I left a school laid out on one city block to start a program at a school situated on a 1,000-acre wildlife preserve. I didn't realize I had left one of the most honest athletics directors for an AD who was not honest.

While I went back to my athletics director at St. Francis to negotiate the four changes in my contract, at the same time I asked for three additions to the job offer I received from UNF. Carlo Tramontozzi was honest when he told me St. Francis couldn't honor my request. John Ratliff, the athletics director at North Florida, told me he would check with the president and get back with me. The next day he told me they'd meet my three requests: a multi-year contract, a courtesy car and paid expenses to the Final Four. I took him at his word and accepted the job in the spring of 1991.

Two days later I was introduced at a news conference as the first basketball coach for the University of North Florida Ospreys. Less than a month later I found out I was deceived. However, at that moment I was packing up the apartment and moving Sandy, who was pregnant with Devin, our second child, and Colin to Jacksonville, Florida. My three years in Brooklyn were more than just growing stages on the court. There were going to be more mouths to feed.

Before my first day on the job at UNF I had one more stop. I was scheduled to work two weeks at the Campbell University basketball camp. It was billed as the oldest and largest basketball camp in the country. More important, it was a good payday. While there, Sandy informed me our car was stolen again. The only twist was some kids called my house and told her they knew where it was. They would take her there if she paid them. I told her to forget about it and let Braica handle it. Later that night Braica went to East New York to find the car. When he found it he called me. It was in such bad shape he suggested I collect the insurance money. That's what we did when we left New York with all of our belongings packed in a U-Haul. We went to New York with two cars and left with none.

My first office at UNF was a little different than the one at St. Francis. The arena was under construction, so I shared an office in the administration building with the women's basketball coach and the track coach. Thank goodness they were great people. Besides, the track coach was always out running anyhow. When all three of us were calling recruits practically elbow to elbow, it sounded like a scene from *Glengarry Glen Ross*, all of us trying to close the deal.

A month into the job, Ratliff came in with my contract. As I looked it over I thought it was someone else's contract. He explained to me the school couldn't give me a multi-year contract. When I asked Ratliff about his request to the president, he just mumbled. I later found an article where he was quoted as saying he told all candidates they would be under a one-year contract. He must have forgotten to call me on that one. Also, he added, I had to solicit for my own courtesy car and raise my own money for Final Four expenses. I learned an important lesson: Never take a job without a signed contract before the news conference. At that point I should have realized it was not going to be a very honest relationship. The hits just kept on coming.

Two years into my tenure, I realized the move to NCAA Division I was not going to occur as soon as it was implied to me. It took almost 15 years before the Ospreys made the move. I had more immediate concerns on my mind, however. Recruiting a team and creating excitement about the program were my first orders of business. Harder than I thought.

I quickly found out Jacksonville is a city divided by its loyalties to Florida, Florida State and the University of Georgia. All they care about is football. The next biggest sport is spring football and, after that, football recruiting.

In the first 60 days I managed to find a core group of basketball junkies in town and hire my staff. That was easy because all three guys on the staff worked for free. There are so many guys who want to get a foot in the door that you could have 50 applicants for a job that paid nothing. It's an amazing mindset. I don't know of any dentist or accountant who would work for free.

Dwight Cooper, my lead assistant, worked at my side for four years. The day I interviewed him we walked around campus and talked for three hours. When we got back to his car I noticed a girl waiting for him. His fiancée sat there the entire time. She definitely needed that kind of patience to be a coach's wife.

One example of his dedication was his first recruiting trip. He was
scheduled to watch a junior college player work out in the evening, but
when the coach shifted the workout to the next morning Dwight called
me. He asked me what he should do. I told him we didn't have enough
money in the budget to get a hotel room, so he should just sleep in his
car, then shower in the locker room at the junior college in the morning.
He did and we signed the player.

After four years he decided college basketball coaching was not
in his blood. Believe me, at that level it had better be in your blood or
you won't last very long. He left coaching and started his own business.
During his time with me he was a tireless worker and a loyal colleague.
He took the same qualities to his company and turned Professional
Placement Resources, a healthcare staffing firm, into a multi-million
dollar business. I always knew he would make it big.

Chris Phelps and Rich Grady were my two other assistants, both
schoolteachers in Jacksonville. Grady moved from New York shortly
before my arrival and actually interviewed for a job with me when I was
at St. Francis. Phelps was a Michigan guy whom I remembered from
my days at Defiance College. All three of them worked extremely hard
during that first year. For their hard work they got a couple of pairs
of K Swiss sneakers. That was our team shoe, but none of the players
wanted to wear them. I struck a deal with them that made sense on the
surface. They were making basketball shoes for the first time and UNF
was a first-year program. A perfect match, except the shoes weren't very
comfortable. At first I forced the players to wear them, but after I wore
them during two consecutive practices my feet hurt so bad I relented. I
still have a dozen pairs left in my closet. I can't even sell them at a garage
sale.

My core group of boosters became the First Hoop Club. It was a fundraising group that helped put on functions such as season ticket parties, a trip to an Orlando Magic game and even a dinner aboard Ted Turner's America's Cup boat. I don't know how much excitement we created in Jacksonville that first year, but I was sure excited.

CHAPTER EIGHT

Basketball and Beaches

Never before had I been in a recruiting situation where I couldn't use current players to help in the process. On the other hand, I could promise everyone I recruited an opportunity for a starting spot. A natural recruiting pitch. We accumulated more than 50,000 miles on our cars that year evaluating players.

I also managed to get a courtesy car deal going. For two weeks. Budget agreed to the deal, but when I brought the first car back after ten days with more than 3,000 miles on it, the company pulled the deal. The only other car deal took place when one of the university's vice presidents donated his car to the athletic department. It was a Dodge K car with close to 200,000 miles on it. It had only an AM radio. Coop and I were the only coaches brave enough to drive it.

On a recruiting trip to the Miami area (a six-hour drive) the air conditioning went out halfway into the trip. By the time we arrived at the recruit's house, we were soaked with perspiration. With sweat beads dripping from my face, I got out of the car and tried to play it cool. But when I couldn't get the drivers side door shut, playing it cool was out of the question. I wondered how Dean Smith would have handled that situation. On the car's last recruiting trip it died and I had to have

Phelps help me tow it back to campus. I think the car is still sitting in the university parking lot as a shrine to all of the miles spent on the road by the first basketball staff.

The recruiting budget was so limited we very rarely spent the night in a hotel. On one trip to the Kansas and Texas junior college regional tournaments, Coop and I ran out of cash. Our only valid credit card was a Texaco gas card. For three days we lived off hot dogs and chips we bought at each gas stop. The hot dogs were the best in Kansas. Must have been the beef!

There were plenty of days and nights on the road, some more memorable than others. Around Christmas I was at the Kissimmee Shootout outside Orlando when my pager went off in my pocket. It was Sandy, who was due with Devin. I jumped in the car and headed home knowing that if she gave birth while I was on the road I would never hear the end of it.

As I had made the turn toward home on I-95 outside Daytona Beach I was pulled over by a state highway patrolman. He looked at me and asked, "Are you auditioning for the Daytona 500?" For once I had a legitimate excuse for my lead foot. I told him my wife was going to have a baby in Jacksonville and I was rushing home to be there. I thought for sure I would not have received a ticket. When he returned to the car he handed me a ticket and gave me the following advice, "Slow down if you want to see the kid." I appreciated the advice, but I could have done without the ticket.

It wasn't until the following week that Sandy gave birth to Devin, during the Michigan-Iowa game in Iowa City on Jan. 9, 1992. If only she had stopped pushing so hard, I would have been able to see the end of overtime when Michigan's Fab Five squeaked by the Hawkeyes. I wish I could have landed a recruiting class like Steve Fisher's at Michigan. But it didn't take long to get back to reality.

The first two players signed at UNF were out of Florida high schools—Chris Sneed, a 6-foot-6 power forward from Jacksonville, and T.L. Latson, a 6-foot-7 lefty from Gainesville. They were the bookends in the paint I wanted to build the program around. Chris, a very intelligent kid who scored above 1100 on his SATs, was thought of by most coaches as a player who could not score enough to play at the Division I level. His grades were so good he came to UNF on an academic scholarship. Though he wasn't a scorer, I noticed he rebounded his ass off. And that's what he did at UNF for four years. His scoring slowly progressed, and he is still playing professionally more than a decade later. That was good sign since I told UNF President Dr. Adam Herbert I would make our program the Duke of Division II. Later I found out UNF academic standards were higher than Duke's.

T.L. was a different type of kid and player. He was a scorer with a nose for the ball. Off the court he wasn't quite the student Sneed was, but he compiled good grades at P.K. Yonge High School in Gainesville, a well-respected high school. His test scores, however, fell below the requirements set forth by the Florida Board of Regents. The requirements covered all the state schools in Florida, but ten percent of the student body could be admitted as an exception. When he was denied admissions I quickly learned that the deal—between the athletic department and the admissions office to admit student-athletes who fell 60-80 points short of the requirement—was off the table. The director of admissions, informed the president would have to sign off on all academic exceptions, said the president would not do it with athletes. The irony was the president had signed off on exceptions for musicians

in UNF's world-renowned jazz program. Of course, that made no sense
to me.

Reluctantly, I informed T.L. he had only one more chance to qualify
for admissions. Before he took the test, I told him that even if he didn't
make it I would have a place for him to go to school. I called my former
boss, Gary Edwards, who moved on to become the head coach at
Charleston Southern University. I told him I had a player for him if he
didn't make his test score. When he asked me who, I said I couldn't tell
him until after the player took the test. Recruiting is a cutthroat business,
even between friends.

The phone call to tell T.L. he was denied from admission to UNF
was one of my toughest. He was crying and couldn't understand how
football players with worse grades could be admitted into the University
of Florida while he was denied. Just another example of football being
king in Florida. I kept my promise to Gary, so T.L. ended up being a four-
year starter at Charleston Southern. He was named the Most Valuable
Player in the Big South Conference his senior year, and is playing
professionally in Puerto Rico. There is no doubt our program would have
gotten off to a great start with Chris and T.L. as the cornerstones.

Recruiting can often put you in awkward positions. And I don't
mean just dealing with AAU coaches or parents who think their sons
should play entire games. The first time I met Lon Kruger, coaching
at the time with the Florida Gators, was more than a bit awkward. I
received a call from Mike Dulugaz, the head coach at P.K. Yonge High
School in Gainesville about one of his players, Clayton Bates, who was a
walk-on with the Gators. I was very interested, but the only way I could
evaluate him was by watching him in a pick-up game with the rest of
the Gator players. Out of respect I placed a call to Coach Kruger to get
his approval. His secretary told me he was out of town for the week, so I

decided to go without talking to him. As I watched the pick-up games he walked in. My first thought was, "What is he doing here? The secretary told me he was out of town for the week." I tried to hide the logo on my shirt, but I couldn't hide the fact that I was the only person in the gym not wearing shorts and sneakers. As he approached I stuck out my hand and introduced myself. After a few uncomfortable moments he asked me if I wanted to talk with the player. I couldn't believe my ears. He helped me recruit one of his own players, albeit a walk-on.

Bates never left Florida, but I did make a friend in Coach Kruger. Later he came to talk at the coach's clinic I ran in Jacksonville. It proved to be a good night after all.

Two other players I lost out on made significant impacts. As mentioned, Sitter was the last player I signed at St. Francis. When I asked Ratliff if I could raise the money for Sitter to come to UNF and sit out for a year, I was told it was not possible. Sitter ended up at New Mexico State for a year, then transferred to UNF for his senior year. He wound up being a Division II All-American.

Mike Frensley would have been our starting point guard had he come back to his native state as I had planned. When we recruited Frensley he told us how badly he wanted to go to a Division I school. Though he was the son of a coach in Florida, he was not recruited by any Division I school in the state. We stuck by him because no one else in the state believed he was Division I caliber. It was a phone call from one of my former assistants that changed things.

Chris Casey, after working for me at St. Francis, became an assistant at St. Peter's College in New Jersey. When he called looking for a point guard, I thought it would be better for our chances if Frensley went to St. Peter's instead of a junior college for another year. I sent Casey a film and he offered Frensley a scholarship. I truly believed that Mike wouldn't like Jersey City and would transfer home to Florida, more specifically to North Florida. I couldn't have been more wrong.

You might remember Mike as the pony-tailed player who hit the game-winning shot on ESPN to send St. Peter's to the NCAA tournament in 1991. He still lives in Jersey City today. I guess he won't be going back to Florida anytime soon.

The breakdown of our first team included six Florida kids, a 26-year-old Swedish transfer from Stetson (in Deland, Fla.), three junior college players, three transfers and a 27-year-old Brazilian named Marcos Santos.

When I first met Marcos he was attending a junior college in Temple Terrace, Florida. I will never forget one of our initial conversations. When I asked him how his English class was going, Marcos told me he was writing a report on "Magical" Johnson. I knew he would be a struggle academically, but he was 6-foot-9 and a good kid. He fell under a unique UNF rule that stated a junior college transfer had to transfer 60 hours or it would revert back to high school grades, regardless of the grade point average in junior college. When Marcos committed we explained to him that he needed to take a couple classes at the local junior college. We added that we would do what we could to help him.

That summer he enrolled in sociology and photography at Florida Community College-Jacksonville (FCCJ). One of our other recruits, Aaron Nichols, was already in town, so they shared an apartment. Marcos was hired as the tallest deliveryman in LaMee florist history. One drawback was he didn't have a driver's license, so when someone drove him to each location, he walked the flowers to the door.

Everything went well until I got a call in the middle of the night from Nichols. He told me Marcos was on the side of his bed threatening to kill himself. I jumped in my car and rushed over. He explained if he didn't pass his classes he would have to go back to his poverty stricken neighborhood in Brazil. He said he would rather die than go home a failure. He then pulled from under the bed a gun he bought at a pawn shop. After convincing him to put away the gun we talked until the sun came up. I assured him I would get him through classes. Talk about pressure. Making a couple free throws was nothing compared to that challenge.

From that point on we met four times a week at the Waffle House for breakfast and I tutored him in sociology. I don't know who was more relieved when he received a passing grade—him or me. He was officially admitted. To this day he is one of my biggest success stories. Later on he became the president of the Weather Channel in South America. He was tragically killed in a motorcycle accident in 2007.

Chris Lee was another success story during my first year at UNF. As part of the process of assembling the team, we wanted to give all local high school players a chance to earn a spot. So we held open tryouts at one of the local middle schools, our only option since there was no gym on campus. Lee was one of almost 100 players who showed up, but he was the only one we kept. A long 6-foot-5 forward, there was just something about him. A year later he earned a spot in the starting lineup on opening night.

I never had a bigger challenge than coaching a program in the first year of its existence. Besides building a team roster from scratch, I had to find a place to play and practice. We played most of our home games at the local junior college, but finding a place to practice was more difficult. We split our time between the middle school and different local high schools. The high school I remember most was The Episcopal School, the one with no air conditioning. Though we practiced at night, the gym temperatures in the gym approached 100 degrees. One night we cut

practice short because Sitter
perspired through his shoes.
When he ran he left puddles
behind, which made the
floor too dangerous. The only
constant about our practices
was taking the practice gear
home to wash. Having done
the laundry at St. Francis for
three years, I had enough
experience to open up my own
laundromat.

Pumping up my team during UNF's first game in the program's history.

We drove vans to our first
game in November 1992, at
Embry-Riddle College. Its arena was under construction, so its home
court was Silver Sands Middle School in Daytona Beach. At least a long
court wouldn't throw us off in our first game. We lost by one point. It
was going to be harder than I thought.

Our schedule was not very good the first year. I scheduled games
with four Division I schools that included a trip to San Diego State for a
tournament. Sandy, as promised, did not make the trip. Since we didn't
have a court to call our own, we played the majority of our games on the
road. We won our last two games while breaking the 100-point mark in
both contests. After winning Coach of the Year honors in my last year
at St. Francis, the only award I would have been considered for at UNF,
finishing the first year with a 7-20 record, was Van Driver of the Year.

The second year, we added a transfer from Stanford, Bobby Patton;
a couple of junior college players; and Sitter, who finally became eligible.
We were 11-3 at the midpoint of the season, averaging close to 90 points

a game. We had three great shooters in Nichols, Sitter and Patton. Our point guard was a transfer from New Jersey by the name of Ricesell Bogan. If the others missed, we always had Sneed in the paint to clean up. Then it happened. In the space of five minutes during our game against crosstown foe, Edward Waters, the season went down the drain. Bogan chipped a bone in his kneecap and Patton tore a ligament in his knee. Both missed the next ten games.

The season hit another low when I got tossed from the Florida Southern game. After the game the Moccasins coach came up to Patton and me telling us he wished he could have played us at full strength. He later got his wish in the Sunshine State Conference tournament.

A few bright spots in the regular season included the play of Sitter who had point totals of 30, 35, 40 and 25, with the game-winner at

Giving instruction to Scott Alford. Scott transferred back from Davidson.

Rollins. Plus, Patton and Bogan returned for the conference tournament. Our first-round opponent was Florida Southern, ranked 17th in the NCAA Division II Poll. That time, at full strength, we won 87-80. Patton, Bogan and Sitter were spectacular. Unfortunately, one more knee injury did us in. During the second half, Sitter tore cartilage in his knee. He was a shell of himself in the semifinal loss to Eckerd. Despite the loss our late-season performance gave us something to build on for the following year. We had went from seven wins to 15 wins, which still stands as the most wins in a season.

For the next two years, the whole turned out to be greater than the sum of its parts. UNF started out 8-0 in 1994-95 behind the play of Patton and another New Mexico State transfer, Darren Jackson. Then we had the trip from hell, part two. It was in Ames, Iowa, for a game against Iowa State, under then-coach Tim Floyd.

Colin and Devin getting some post game shooting practice at UNF Arena.

To save money we flew into Kansas City and rented a couple of vans for the three-and-a-half-hour drive. We wanted to save some of the guarantee money we received from playing the game. In retrospect, I should have spent the extra money. We got caught in a snowstorm and didn't pull into the hotel until 2 in the morning. The next night the game was a blur until I screamed at the official, pleading not to give one of their players every call. Of course, I am leaving out a couple of descriptive adjectives. The player in question was Fred "The Mayor" Hoiberg, who unfortunately for us happened to be one of the most popular players in Cyclone history. You would have thought I insulted God. It was the first time I was afraid in a gym. We lost the game by double digits and, more important, we lost our momentum. After losing our next game I was forced to make a stand.

In the middle of a film session the team's leading scorer, Darren Jackson, stood up and walked out. He mumbled something about not sacrificing for the team anymore. To say I was caught off balance was an understatement. I ignored him and finished the film session. That was the beginning of the end for Jackson as a member of the team. When I spoke to him, he was even more defiant. After meeting with the team captains, I was informed of things I was unaware of concerning cancerous actions in the locker room. The team voted 11-0 against Jackson returning to the team.

When the newspapers ran the story it became front page news, which did not make the UNF president very happy. As fate would have it, when attending a Super Bowl party the next day, I happened to be sitting with the UNF president, Dr. Adam Herbert. He was always interested in the basketball program. During the first year recruiting I could count on a phone call every Monday night from him. The questions were always the same: "Who are you involved with in recruiting? Is he any good?" I thought the second question was strange. Why would I purposely recruit a bad player? Anyhow, he was very supportive about the Jackson incident, but I knew he also wanted to win. Most of all he didn't want any more negative publicity.

I kicked Darren off the team, a tough decision since he was not only our leading scorer but one of the leading scorers in the country. I told myself it would help set the tone for the future. In retrospect I might have handled it differently. As a coach you are also an educator and you can't educate someone if you get rid of him. Maybe I've mellowed with age.

At the same time, I had to dismiss another Osprey starter for violation of team rules. We went into our next game without two starters. That night we battled Florida Tech down to the final second. We held a one-point lead when one of Florida Tech's players threw in a desperation shot from behind the backboard for the 80-79 win. That night I walked out with my head held high knowing the kids came together and played their hearts out. I didn't know the lack of confidence from that loss would haunt us the rest of the year. A month passed before we won another game.

Patton went off for 35 points against Barry University in a road win. I couldn't have been any happier for anyone that night. He transferred from Stanford University the previous year because he did not want to sit behind future NBA guard Brevin Knight. In the beginning he really struggled to mesh with the new players. A call from his father at Christmas time and the dismissal of Jackson helped turn his season around.

His father, Bob Patton Sr., a high school coach in Ohio, was a no-nonsense guy to say the least. When he called me I didn't know what to expect. The norm was a parent making an excuse for their son. I learned a long time ago it didn't matter what level of competition you're talking about. I can still remember Derrick Chievous' mother screaming at Don Nelson, the coach of the Golden State Warriors, after a game. She felt he wasn't playing her son enough minutes. The call from Coach Patton was completely the opposite. He told me to send Bobby home if he kept whining and playing poorly. He must have said the same thing to his son because in the second half of the season his play picked up dramatically.

A couple of years later I received a letter from Bobby explaining what was on his mind. He also apologized for his screwed-up thinking. He ended up graduating from Stanford. That's right, Stanford. Stanford head coach Mike Montgomery made a deal that if Patton took classes at another school when he transferred, he had the option of returning. Stanford accepted those classes as part of the deal and paid for an extra semester in order for Patton to graduate with a Stanford degree. So Stanford kept its graduation record intact. A school pays for a former player who had not been there in two years, while we were operating on only four full scholarships. That's why every coach wants to get to the big time.

At the end of the year, since Sandy was pregnant with Kailey, our third child, I was looking for an additional source of income. I had been running camps since the day I started the program, but salaries at the Division II level didn't rise as fast as Division I. My associate head coach, Dwight Cooper, introduced me to one of the best moneymakers outside basketball. Coop moved up from an assistant to associate head coach one summer when he gave himself that title in our camp brochure. When I asked the athletics director after the fact, he said it was okay as long as he knew he wasn't getting a raise.

In the summer of 1995, fireworks tents littered both sides of the road in the state of Florida ten days before the Fourth of July. The previous year Coop ran one. I scoffed at him until he told me how much he made, then I lobbied to pitch a tent in Atlantic Beach. It was a prime location and only a couple miles from my house. Usually civic groups run them as a fundraiser. I planned to run mine as a fundraiser as well. The Zvosec Children's Scholarship Fund.

For nine days I sat in the tent hawking fireworks. Every morning I unloaded the van borrowed from UNF and set up the tables. Then each night I broke it down. Those were 12-hour days. Most of the time I worked alone. My only break was when Sandy came down with the kids and gave me a few minutes to run to the bathroom. The last couple of days I hired a few of my players. Aaron Nichols was the best at selling. He uses the same enthusiasm today as a high school basketball coach. We sold what was delivered and returned the rest. Each tent earned 20 percent of the total sold. A good week would clear $6,000-$8,000. I did that for four years and always had a good week. By the end my new assistants were running tents of their own. My timing was perfect because the summer I left fireworks were banned in Florida because of a drought at the time. It turned out to be very profitable for the Zvosec fund.

Season four (1995-96) marked a big change for the North Florida Ospreys. We changed athletics directors and I changed my assistant. Coop left to start his own business and I hired Joe Carey based on a recommendation from one of my closest friends, Ken Dempsey. The change in athletics directors was a positive one, while the change in assistants would be the opposite.

We also switched from driving vans to a minibus, so I had to obtain a commercial driver's license. The school actually owned a full-sized bus, but our budget didn't support the gas expense and the driver hiring. Driving a minibus was not as bad as it sounded after driving vans the previous three years. Also, it meant turning the driving over to my new assistant, Joe Carey. That turned out to be a major mistake.

On his first trip he backed into my car. Then on our only overnight trip he tore off part of the minibus's roof on a hotel canopy. That left a big hole in the roof and, of course, it rained on the way home. Fortunately, the women's basketball team had left some feminine hygiene products on the bus, which we used to stuff in the hole and stop the leak. That was the last game my assistant attended due to a stomach problem. All I know is I should have been the one with an ulcer.

Through it all we played pretty well and made it to the conference tournament championship game. If we won we would have advanced to the NCAA Division II tournament. It also meant that I would have received a $1000 bonus from Reebok, the only incentive clause in my contract. I think the shoe rep put it in for us to keep buying the shoes and thought it was a safe bet. We had a losing record the previous year, so the rep thought we had no chance to improve enough to advance to the Division II tournament.

In the first round game it took a great defensive play by Jesse Hudson and two free throws by Phil Caple to upset Rollins. Hudson took a charge with less than 30 seconds left in the game. The official nullified the basket, preserving the Ospreys' one-point lead. Caple then iced the game at the line. Against Eckerd in the semis, Chris Sneed was unstoppable. He recorded a double-double to lift UNF to the championship game against Florida Southern. Not bad for a guy many thought couldn't score.

Plotting strategy during a time out at UNF.

In the championship game we led most of the game in front of a partisan Florida Southern crowd. The game was played in Lakeland, its home site, but it was like a morgue in there. With less than a minute to go and clinging to a two-point lead, my two best players collided going after an offensive rebound. As a Cleveland Browns fan, I'll never forget The Drive or The Fumble. To me that moment will always be called The Collision. Sneed, voted the tourney MVP, was knocked senseless for the last minute. Chris Patterson, the game's leading scorer, broke a bone above his eye finishing him for the night. We had one last chance to win, but the three-pointer was off the mark. That year proved what a strong senior class could do for a program. When seniors make plays you win games.

Heart to heart with Chris Sneed. One of my all time favorites.

My last year at UNF was filled with the growing pains brought on by starting three freshmen. One freshman, Ian Foster, in particular stood a little straighter than the others. He looked like Opie Taylor, but played like an assassin. He made 18 straight free throws on his way to a 42-point night in the first round of the conference tournament. But the irony is that if I had seen him in person as a high school senior I doubt that I would have taken him.

A friend of mine in Indiana sent me a tape on Foster. I immediately liked the way he could score. When I called to ask about Foster, my friend told me Foster would be even better when he got his back brace off. I was stunned. I rewatched the tape and still didn't notice the brace that kept Foster from bending over. So much for the science of recruiting. Sometimes when you have an opportunity to see a player numerous times you start looking for flaws. In this case distance made the heart grow fonder. Thank goodness for friends and videotape.

Two other players we signed resulted from the San Francisco earthquake in 1989. With a limited recruiting budget, we had to improvise. Coop's wife was an insurance claims adjuster, so when the earthquake struck she was sent to California to work for six months. Part of the compensation was a ticket for her husband to fly out and visit her. Coop did and spent his time watching a couple junior college players. Eventually, we signed both of them.

Some games stand out in your mind forever. One was during the 1995-96 season at Savannah State University in Georgia, which had an old gym with windows just below the roofline at the end of the court. The windows were left open to cool the building. When it started to rain they couldn't shut them, so water collected beyond the baseline. Players had to stand in puddles to inbound the ball. One of the janitors theorized baby powder would soak up the water. After we slipped for the fifth time on the failed mixture, an official came over to my bench and asked if I wanted the game stopped. I looked at the score (we were up by eight) and thought, "I don't want to make this trip back up here." So I told him we'd keep playing. We ended up losing, 65-63, on a half court shot at the buzzer. I should have followed the *Bull Durham* pattern and accepted the rainout. (A couple of years later we were awarded a forfeit win when it was discovered Savannah State played an ineligible player.)

Another memorable trip was the return from Florida Southern. After we got our clocks cleaned, I wanted to race home as fast as I could. A little too fast. We were a couple miles from the exit when a cop pulled me over and ticketed me. The fine was doubled because it was a work zone. It cost me $200. When I got back on the bus the players knew better. No one said a word. To add insult to injury Sandy and Colin, my oldest son, were still up when I got home. He was so excited because he got the chance to listen to the game on the radio. Unfortunately, the first words out of his mouth were, "You lost and Daddy you ain't much of a coach." After a few seconds I did what a good parent should do. I told him not to use the word "ain't."

By my sixth year at UNF, I grew tired of the amount of time I spent fundraising and promoting. Not that I disliked it, but it took me away from coaching and teaching. However, public relations work allowed me to meet some great people.

One in particular was Ash Verlander. He was the founder of AHL, a big insurance company in Jacksonville. When I told him about the money we needed, he stepped up and suggested a luncheon with the ten biggest money people in Jacksonville. He called his friends and the meeting was set. We had the top people from First Union Bank, CSX, Bell South and Winn-Dixie to name a few. However, when the vice president of development caught wind of the proposed luncheon, the proverbial shit hit the fan.

Next thing I knew the president ordered me to call off the luncheon. What was I supposed to do? Insult one of the most powerful men in town or get fired for alienating my president? The luncheon was called off, but to Ash's credit he still followed through with his donations. Thanks Ash!!

Each fall I took my team to work the concession stand at the Jacksonville Jaguars football games. You may have seen me or some of my players on television. We were the beer guys going up and down the stands. At first I had to persuade the players to come, but after one of them received a $100 tip from a thirsty, obviously drunk, fan it was easy to convince them to go back.

Another big fundraiser I started was the Hooters Shootout. Each year during The Players Championship on the PGA Tour we put up a hoop at the Hooters in Ponte Vedra Beach. For $50 contestants shot free throws against me. If they won, they got $50. We made close to $5,000 every year. A big thanks to the Hooters girls for pushing contestants our way.

We even had some of the PGA Tour pros take part. I will be forever a Dudley Hart fan due to the amount of money he dropped at the shootout. I am proud to say I lost on only two occasions. Once to a woman in high heels, Donna Geils at the time and now WNBA President Donna Orender. I found out later she was a college basketball standout at Queens College before playing professional basketball. She let me keep the money. Hey, any way to make a buck.

Over the years I received quite a few letters from former players or parents to express their gratitude. I always appreciated their kind words. I hoped I treated their son how I would want my own kids to be treated. That is not to say everyone was happy. The strangest letter I received came from a college coach whose son I was recruiting. When I left, he felt compelled to write me about how much of a scumbag I was for taking another job. I never really understood his motives since his son had not played for me, nor had he ever committed to play for me. I guess he was having a bad day and needed a release. I hope I provided it for him.

That same year I received a letter from a father named Brian Haney regarding his son. Brian Haney's life had been a favorite camp story I told for years even though I had never met the man. I borrowed the story from Pete Gillen when he told it at Notre Dame's camp because Brian Haney's life was a lesson in perseverance. Haney was cut from his high school team the first three years. In his senior year he finally made the team and ended up scoring two points. Then he went from scoring two points in high school to playing college basketball in Canada (where he was named in his senior year the MVP of Canadian college basketball). Eventually he ended up playing in the NBA briefly for the Philadelphia 76ers. A player who scored only two points in his high school career. Simply amazing! Finally I was going to meet him because his son Brian Haney Jr. was looking to transfer from the College of Charleston. On the younger Haney's visit we talked about his father and how his life story had influenced the both of us. He had a desire to transfer to UNF, but after I took a job at Millersville University, Haney decided to go elsewhere. I know I've said it before, but it really is a small world.

At the beginning of my last season in 1996-97, I decided that in order to fulfill my goal of returning to the Division I level, I needed to get back up north where most of my contacts were. That spring I was hired as the head coach at Millersville in Pennsylvania, a good Division II job outside Philadelphia. Dr. Gene Carpenter was the athletics director and football coach who hired me. I was his last hire because he relinquished his AD duties shortly after I came on board. The change in leadership altered the vision of the athletic department dramatically. It also meant I would be working for a new boss, Dr. Dan Audette. Not a good situation to be in.

The coach I replaced, John Cochan, was very successful on the court but ran into some problems off the court. He was dismissed for failing to graduate players and committing some minor NCAA violations. He left behind some talented young players and a disgruntled assistant.

John Wilson, an assistant at Millersville for almost ten years, was a finalist for the head coaching position. The president, however, was not going to hire him because of his connection with the previous head coach. On the other hand he told me I had to keep him on my staff. That presented a dilemma. Knowing how badly he wanted the job, I also knew he was hurt by not getting it. I tried to work it out with him, but we both knew it wasn't going to happen. He lasted a year, then resigned. It taught me a valuable lesson about keeping someone you don't know from a previous staff: You don't do it! I am happy to say a few years later we patched things up after running into each other at the Final Four.

CHAPTER NINE

Transitional Year

When I took the UNF job I truly believed I had found my dream job. I remember talking with my first boss, Gary Edwards, about being a head coach at a Division I school near the beach. Convinced at first that UNF would be elevated to the Division I level in a couple of years, I had second thoughts after learning that the president of UNF was elected the head of the NCAA President's Council as a Division II rep. When it was apparent the move would not happen, it was time to work my way back up. UNF was not going to lead me there.

Once again it was time to load up the moving van, the third time I moved the family. Sandy and I packed up the furniture, loaded the truck and headed north. At the Division II level you don't receive moving expenses that cover the cost of a professional moving company, so the Zvosec movers sprang into action. Sandy followed behind with Devin and Kailey while Colin rode with me. We drove through the night. While Sandy and the two kids with her stopped in Baltimore, Colin and I headed for Millersville.

We arrived around midnight and went to bed in the house I rented from the university while I looked for permanent housing. I woke up the next morning to find Colin gone. He got up in the middle of the night to get a drink out of the truck. The door to the house shut behind him and locked. I was still sleeping, so I didn't hear the knocking. A couple of coeds found him locked out on the porch the next morning and took him to their house for breakfast. He was so excited about the pancakes it was easy to convince him not to tell his mother. That was until the next day when I had to tell his mother why a couple of college girls walking by knew his name.

My tenure at Millersville lasted 15 months. I was able to lead the team into the league playoffs as was the custom under the previous regime and at the same time re-establish credibility off the court with the community. Also, it was a good year because Colin was old enough to attend camp.

I even took him on a couple recruiting trips. One Friday I took him to the Sonny Hill league at Temple University. A couple hours before the first game, someone was tragically shot inside the gym. As we walked in the gym Colin was oblivious to the yellow police tape cordoning off the area. He started to walk right through it until a cop grabbed him. I explained the situation to him, then told him if he ever wanted to go with me again he couldn't tell his mother. I don't think he ever did.

CHAPTER TEN

Life-Changing Phone Call

As I prepared to start my second year in the fall of 1998, I placed a phone call that changed my career once again. My former assistant at St. Francis, Chris Casey, just left his position at St. Peter's to take another job. When I called on a Wednesday to congratulate him, the head coach, Roger Blind, answered the phone. Our conversation drifted to possible replacements. At that point he asked me if I were interested, then suggested a meeting two days later.

After hanging up I weighed all the pros and cons. In the process of hiring a new assistant, I wasn't given a final say. That was a big negative. Can you imagine? The athletics director formed a committee to hire my assistant. I guess I should be thankful I had a vote like the other four people on the committee. When I was told I couldn't interview my graduate assistant (Mark Burke), I almost quit on the spot. As I drove up to Jersey City on that Friday, I was ready to say yes if the job were offered.

We spoke for a few minutes, then he offered and I accepted. That was easy, but I had to figure out how that was going to work with my family. Over the weekend I put the big recruiting pitch on my wife and how it would be a great move for us. She had heard that line a few too many times. We finally agreed I could take the job, but the family would stay behind in Millersville for the school year. Sandy didn't want to move the kids into another school. Plus, she loved it there. It was a nice community and only an hour and change from her family.

The following Tuesday, we held Midnight Madness on the Millersville campus. The administration had been informed by then, so I was asked to act as if nothing happened until they could get a replacement. I agreed. In retrospect, I shouldn't have done it. It made me look bad to my players. I managed to avoid the reporters after Midnight Madness. I didn't want to be quoted about the upcoming season since I wasn't going to be there. An assistant still hadn't been hired by then, so my graduate assistant told the reporters I was in the locker room as I slipped out the back door. That left me with an uncomfortable feeling, but I didn't want to say something that could be thrown back in my face. I felt awful for the players, but I knew my relationship with the Millersville athletics director would be a constant distraction during the season. He and I disagreed on just about everything.

That Friday I drove up to St. Peter's, a Division I member of the Metro Atlantic Athletic Conference (MAAC), to take part in the Peacocks' Midnight Madness. I was probably the only coach that year to go through two separate opening practices. As part of my deal at St. Peter's I was allowed to stay in a furnished apartment on campus reserved for visiting priests. It was a nice place, but had no cable television.

I stayed on campus the first part of the year and I went home only on our days off from practice. Though I was back on the Division I level, I definitely paid a price. It was tough at home, but I was hopeful it wouldn't last long. I decided that once the games started I would drive back and forth every day. Hey, it was only a two-and-a-half hour commute each way.

A typical day started by leaving the house at the crack of dawn, then returning around midnight. Three things saved me on the road that year - a cell phone, low gas price and police card. The cell phone helped me fulfill my recruiting responsibilities. I made my phone calls and wrote down some of my notes before I got home. (It was much easier talking on the phone and driving than writing and driving.) The price of gas kept me from going bankrupt. I once filled up my car for 88 cents per gallon. The police card given to me by my brother-in-law (a policeman in Lorain) got me out of a number of speeding tickets. I felt like a postal carrier because neither rain nor snow kept me from making it to practice. I drove through a snowstorm once only to find out practice was cancelled. The rest of the staff couldn't make it in from a half-hour away. Since I was there I had the players walk across the street to shoot. If I could brave the blizzard they could, too.

The job at St. Peter's was a big risk. Not only was I accepting a sizable pay cut, but my family was without health insurance because it cost too much. The biggest gamble was whether or not I'd be employed at the end of the year. The head coach was in the final year of his contract. On top of that, he lost the last ten games the previous year. Most of my friends in the business thought I was crazy. I saw it as an opportunity to get back to the Division I level. It was worth the risk!

The first couple months I was in basketball heaven. It was the first time in my career I worked on a staff with another full-time assistant. We actually had daily staff meetings. In the past I had staff meetings, but by myself or with one other guy. At St. Peter's we spent up to three hours a day in front of the chalkboard going over practice plans. Couple that with my workouts at night with the players and I was like a kid in a candy store. Working out the players gave me a new lease on life. It was something I really missed when I became a head coach. I vowed that when I became head coach again I would never let my other responsibilities take me away from the individual workouts with my players.

Recruiting at St. Peter's also proved to be a unique experience. The first day the other assistant, Bill Maranz, came into the office with a $100 roll of stamps. My first thought was he had a big Christmas card list. It turned out that to send recruits a daily note we had to use our own stamps. That was the first school where I wore out my tongue licking stamps.

Bringing in recruits for visits was also an adventure. We had different routes from the airport depending on the time of day. One day it didn't help. We had a recruit and his parents on campus when a half-dozen police cars zipped by with their sirens blasting. I looked at Bill and asked him what movie they were filming today. He didn't miss a beat as he rattled off every film shot in Jersey City.

Being away from home for long periods gave me a new appreciation for Sandy and her hard work raising the kids. She was a real trooper even though I know there were days she cussed me up a storm. When I came home I made sure to spend quality time with the kids. I also took each of my sons up to St. Peter's to spend the weekends. On one such trip I thought I was going to lose my job.

We played an exhibition game that I brought my youngest son, Devin, to see. When the game started I made sure the manager kept an eye on him at the end of the bench. The first half went fine. With a couple of minutes left in the game I looked down to the end of the bench and Devin was nowhere to be found. As I started to walk down I turned to see Devin standing next to the head coach, who was crouching in front of the scorers table. I was mortified. I was there only a couple of months. What would his reaction be? I saw him say something to Devin, then Devin turned to walk back to the bench. Thank goodness we were in the closing moments of a game that had already been decided. After the game I apologized to Coach Blind and asked him what he had said. He told me Devin wanted to know if he could go get a lollipop from the office. Glad to see his head was in the game.

The season started without the services of our starting center, who had broken a bone in his hand. Jake Holmes, the kind of kid who really wanted to play, would do anything he was told if it meant becoming a better player. To help his hand heal I brought him two gallons of milk every couple of days. The girl in the grocery store must have thought I was nuts when I told her what I was doing. We also developed a one-handed workout he and I did everyday. By the fifth game he was given clearance to play. That was the good news.

The bad news was we dropped our first four games and the players were beginning to wonder if St. Peter's would ever win. Since I hadn't been there the previous year, I was able to keep things going in a positive direction though we weren't winning. At night some of the players came by my apartment to talk about the game and life in general. For the first time in a while I felt like I made an impact on kids. Once we won our first conference game things started to take off. It's funny how confidence is such a fragile thing. It takes only one victory or one loss to make or break it.

We finally started to click on the court. Off the court I was getting to know every radio talk show host intimately. The purpose of driving back and forth every day was a small attempt to help out at home so my wife could get away in the morning to run before I left. It might have been the only thing that kept her from either killing or divorcing me. One other idea I tried, however, really backfired. Since I was gone on her birthday, I decided to have a singing gorilla deliver the cake. When the gorilla tried to hug her she flipped the cake at him. I am glad it was him and not me. I never tried that again.

The team had some bumps in the road, such as the night one of our best players hurt his knee. I was in my apartment after the game when I got a call from his roommate. It was about 3 in the morning and his knee was killing him. So I took him to the hospital and waited for his mother to come. She took the train over from the Bronx. It turned out that he had a reaction to the anti-inflammatory pills the doctor gave him after the game. I was glad I was able to help. Being there for the players is what makes coaching so satisfying.

The 1999 MAAC tournament was held in Buffalo that year. In the first round we upset the home team, Canisius. In the semis we beat Niagra, another local favorite. That matched us against Siena in the championship game on ESPN, one game away from making the NCAA tournament.

Over the years I developed some superstitions around tournament time. The year we made it to the conference championship at UNF, we started each practice leading up to the tournament with all of the players lying on the floor with a bag over their heads. They must have thought I lost my mind. The thinking was that each day we cleaned out the bad thoughts and replaced them with positive vibes. I passed around an Irish worry stone for each player to rub out the bad karma, then had them rub a medallion that read "Winning With Teamwork." That was supposed to lock in the good karma. We repeated the same ritual in the locker room before the first round game. By the championship game the players were asking me for the stone and medallion.

At St. Peter's my superstition was not as pronounced. I doubt the head coach would have let me put bags over the players' heads. The first night I threw a nickel in the fountain at the hotel. One of the players saw me and asked for a nickel. He did the same thing. By the third night I had all of the players asking for a nickel before we went over to the game.

We lost the championship game to the Paul Hewitt-coached Siena Saints. It was his last game at Siena and mine at St. Peter's. He moved on to Georgia Tech. I was looking for another job as an assistant coach. Maybe we should have thrown quarters into the fountain.

Coach Blind received a well-deserved extension at the end of the season. He is one of the good guys in the business and I will be forever in his debt. Though I enjoyed my year at St. Peter's I couldn't afford to stay another year. I still lived that vow of poverty the Catholic priests take. Also, Sandy was not too keen on the idea of moving to Jersey City.

In the spring of 1999 I took a job as assistant coach at American University for Art Perry. I believed it was a good move on many fronts. My salary ($45,000) almost matched what I made at Millersville. There was some job security (Art, as an alum, had two years left on his contract). And we were closer to Sandy's family. It was the sixth state (counting the District of Columbia) out of ten on the eastern seaboard where I coached. Only four to go.

I commuted that spring from our house in Pennsylvania. It was only a 90-minute drive if you hit the traffic just right. On the bright side, it was an hour shorter than my one-way drive to Jersey City. I jumped right into the recruiting fray and wound up signing Reggie Bryant out of Baltimore. He played his high school basketball at Calvert Hall for Mark Amatucci, my old boss at Loyola College. My new boss was excited about the signing since Reggie was an all-star in the tough Baltimore Catholic League.

Two weeks later it fell apart as Reggie failed a math course and consequently wasn't admitted. I didn't want to give up, so I met with his family, his high school coach and the head coach at St. Thomas More prep school. It was set. Attend the prep school in the fall, then American University the following year. It was supposed to be an open-and-shut case. I failed to understand the coach at St. Thomas More had quite a few coaching friends. When Reggie started to play well he opened up his recruiting to schools at higher levels. So much for sticking to your word.

Recruiting is a business that depends on relationships. My feeling is when you help a player, there needs to be some reciprocity. In that case we helped Bryant make the connection at St. Thomas More; therefore, we should have been his first choice the following year. Many prep school coaches and junior college coaches will do whatever they can to make sure that happens. To me that was only fair since we were the ones to lend Bryant a helping hand. Others, as I found out the hard way, will look out only for their own interest. Bryant signed at Villanova.

Some head coaches are known to fire assistants if they don't land players. Thank goodness Art Perry was not one of them. He had been through the recruiting wars at Maryland and understood the game very well. The rest of the staff was made up of ascending young guys. Kevin Broadus, now the head coach at Binghamton, was a D.C. guy and is now a future coaching star. Billy Donlon, the son of a coach, was a great player at UNC-Wilmington. There is no doubt he will be a head coach someday soon. It was a tremendous group of guys.

After taking almost two months to find a new place, we settled on Rockville, Maryland. It was about 15 to 30 minutes from the school. We packed up the kids, loaded the truck and were off again, another move by the Zvosec moving company. That was Sandy's sixth house since we got married in 1989. At least it gave us an excuse to hold plenty of garage sales. It also provided plenty of furniture for my former players. My old furniture is spread across the country.

We settled into a row home across the street from a huge park. It was a great set-up for my kids. There were two basketball courts, one for serious pick-up games and the other for shooting around with my sons. One day, watching a pick-up game, two players caught my eye. A coach is always looking for players. One of the guys on the side told me that one guy was Lonny Baxter who played for the Maryland national championship team in 2002. I really do have an eye for talent.

The other guy caught my attention for another reason. He looked very familiar. When the game ended he walked over and I realized it was Jerry Noll, the player from Cleveland I coached in my last year at UNF. He shot as well on the outdoor court as he did indoors. As it turned out his girlfriend lived down the street. He updated me on his life in the couple years since, then asked if I could help him play professionally overseas. I called a couple agents and, sure enough, he played a couple years overseas. Fate is a funny thing.

Our season was just as surprising. We never seemed to get over the hump. We won a couple, lost a couple. We had good players who weren't quite as coachable as the ones at St. Peter's. Maybe that was my fault because I was never able to develop the same type of relationships as the previous year. Don't get me wrong. They weren't bad kids. They just had too many outside people in their ears and other ideas in their minds. One player in particular stands out.

Ron Hearns, a talented player, was the son of the famous boxer, Thomas "Hitman" Hearns. I thought he was dedicated to basketball, but he always seemed to have something else on his mind. Hearns went on to have a solid career at AU, but I think he could have been much better if he were more focused. After graduation, he followed in father's footsteps and became a professional boxer. The last time I checked he was still undefeated. I guess he found his true passion.

We played in the opening round of the Patriot League tournament against East Carolina University. At the tournament banquet the other assistant showed me an article in the *Washington Post* about us being fired, quoting an unnamed source (Deep Throat, I suppose). I had heard rumblings about our job security, but still believed if we won the opening round game we would be okay. Everyone liked Coach Perry, and we had increased our win total that year. Also, we were going to have everybody back from a team that advanced in the conference tournament three years in a row. Besides, his predecessor had six straight losing seasons. When we won the first game, I felt pretty good about our future.

The next night we played George Mason University, coached by Larranaga. A few years before I had talked with him about a job on his staff when he was the head coach at Bowling Green, but I couldn't take the pay cut at the time. After we lost the second round game, the athletics director grabbed Coach Perry by the arm coming off the court. After he talked to the team Perry told me the AD wanted to see him in his office on Sunday. We both knew what that meant.

Firing a coach is part of college basketball. The method of carrying it out is the unbelievable part. Some guys return to their offices to find a note on their chair, others are fired over the phone or by e-mail. I am amazed so many administrators lack the tact and integrity to carry it out in a professional manner.

If I were an AD, I would set up a meeting at the end of the season to evaluate the program. In what is supposed to be an academic environment, it only makes sense then to do it in a way that will provide an educational experience for both parties. If the coach didn't meet a predetermined set of criteria, then his contract would not be renewed. Most ADs won't even give a coach a written set of criteria. Those who do don't always stick to them. Also, if an AD were obligated to reimburse the university for any money owed to a coach, the AD would think twice about firing a coach. As I have always said, "I love the coaching profession, but I hate the business."

Unlike the athletics director, Coach Perry displayed his class on the way home to D.C. from the tournament. When the players asked for something to eat, he took them to a nice restaurant. Even though he knew he was fired on the two-hour bus ride home. To the end he gave the players a positive educational experience.

The following morning I flew to Kansas for a junior college tournament. Though I had a pretty good idea what was going to happen, I felt it was my responsibility to continue working. My phone rang that afternoon and Coach Perry informed me that we were fired. It was the first time in 18 years that I had been fired or part of a staff that had been fired. Around that time Billy Herion, the head coach at East Carolina, consoled me. Almost a decade later I still remember the first person I talked with after I learning I was fired. Encouraging me, Herion said not to worry. With my background he felt I would have no problem getting another job.

On the flight home my mind raced with thoughts about the future. The first order of business was finding out how long I remained on the payroll at American University. The assistant AD informed me I would be paid until the end of April, giving me a month to find a job. Two weeks later the locks were changed on the AU office doors. I guess the administrators were afraid the coaching staff would steal the paper clips.

After returning home I had to convince Sandy everything would be okay. It was easier said than done since she wasn't working and we had three kids to feed. But after spending time at home I realized she worked harder with the kids than she would have in a paid position. For the first time in my life I filed for unemployment compensation.

Every day I spent my time on the phone contacting anybody who had an opening. I applied for 31 coaching openings over two months. I lost count on the number of coaches who didn't bother to call me back. I made a vow at that time that if I were ever in a position to hire someone I would extend the courtesy of a returned phone call. As the end of April approached I started to question how I was going to pay the bills.

Growing up and throughout my coaching career I never had a lot of money, but I always believed if we needed money it would show up. My parents used to say God will provide. Well I needed Him to provide real quick. That weekend my sister-in-law invited us up to Baltimore for a cookout. I was not in the mood, but knew it would get Sandy out of the house.

At the cookout I ran into an old colleague from my days at Loyola College, Jerry Vignola, formerly the assistant athletics director. He moved on to become the director of several fitness centers in Washington and Baltimore. He offered me a temporary job filling in at the fitness centers. That gave me more time to find another coaching position.

The following Monday I went to work at the Department of Commerce fitness center. It was an easy job and it gave me the free time to call and research coaching openings all day. Of course, when a member asked me for some fitness advice, I provided it. My favorite advice was telling the members to work out for more than 20 minutes. I read somewhere that after 20 minutes the body burned fat at a higher rate. Sounded good to me and it actually worked for the members.

Two other opportunities presented themselves at the same time. The first was submitting stories and jokes to *Readers Digest*. I must have sent them a year's worth of stories. For all of my hard work I received $100. I guess I wasn't as funny as I thought.

The other opportunity was a role in a movie. Do you remember the subway passenger in *Along Came A Spider?* I was the one standing next to Monica Potter (I guess she was the star of the scene) on the platform waiting for the train. That was my acting debut. How about the FBI agent? (Sorry, that scene got cut from the movie.) Ever wonder how movie stars act off-camera? Well, Morgan Freeman was the nicest guy in the world, while his co-star, Monica Potter, definitely had a bad day. I made $235 for a day's work. Not exactly Bruce Willis type money.

CHAPTER ELEVEN

Kansas City, Here I Come

I t wasn't until the first of July that I heard about an assistant coaching job with the UMKC Kangaroos. A close friend, Art Luptkowski, told me a good friend of his, Dean Demopoulos, was named the head coach. I knew Dean a little bit from talking with him about a player who was leaving Temple. The player's decision came down to Millersville and American International College where Luptkowski was the head coach. The player ended up going to AIC. Now I understand why. Luptkowski called Dean on my behalf and we met at the Philadelphia airport. While driving to the ABCD Camp, we talked the whole way like we were old friends. He spent most of the day talking with other people at the camp. Each coach had someone to recommend, but I must have done something right because he offered me the job on the ride home. Knowing my acting days were limited, I accepted.

It was the fifth time I traced a job back to one of my camp connections. The initial connection at ACC and St. Francis was the Mason Dixon camp, Loyola was the Notre Dame camp, UNF was the Virginia camp and UMKC was the Pocono Invitational camp. To this day when someone asks me the best way to get into coaching I tell them to work summer camps. It did wonders for my career.

That move was significant in several ways. It was my fifth school
in five years, but the first time hiring a moving company. With three
kids, there was too much stuff collected. Also, it was the first time
Sandy entrusted me to find a place to live. It also meant Colin would
be attending his fourth elementary school in five years. Kansas City was
a part of the country where neither of us had lived. I convinced her
that the weather was like Baltimore. Unfortunately, when she made her
first trip to K.C. in August, the city was in the midst of 22 straight days
with 100-degree temperatures. Most important, it was another potential
Division I head coaching opportunity.

I had ten days to find a place to rent before heading back to
Rockville to pick up Sandy and the kids. It should have been easy.
How hard could it be to find a house in a major metropolitan area?
Demopolous did it in four hours. The house he bought was closer to the
University of Kansas in Lawrence than to UMKC in the heart of the city. I
wanted something a little closer.

It was difficult because July was a live recruiting period. That meant
I would be on the road the whole month. First, there was a recruiting
trip to the Jerry Mullen Junior College Showcase in Tulsa. A coach at the
University of Missouri in Columbia would fly, but I was still coaching at
a school with a hyphenated name, which meant driving for four hours.
I left Kansas City diligently prepared with enough background on the
Kangaroos to intelligently sell the program. I picked up a shirt from the
bookstore, then got the directions on Mapquest. One thing I didn't check
was the gas gauge. An hour into the trip I was sitting on the side of the
road with an empty gas tank. I didn't know anybody, so I started walking.
About a mile up the road was a house where the lady inside was kind
enough to give me a lift to the gas station. As I filled the tank she asked
me if I was the new coach at UMKC. I sheepishly admitted I was. It's not

like I could deny it - I had a UMKC Kangaroo logo on my shirt. As she
pulled away she wished me good luck. Actually, she said she hoped I was
a better coach than I was a driver.

After the showcase was over, I continued my house search. I thought
it would be a lot easier in K.C. than in D.C., but it turned out to be the
opposite. There were plenty of houses to buy, but not many to rent at
a reasonable price. With five jobs in five years, buying a house was out
of the question. Finally, on my way to another appointment, I spotted
a For Rent sign on the corner. I turned around and went to that house.
After some haggling with the owner we agreed on a price. I thought it
was a pretty good sales job on my part. It turned out the owner was a
nightmare. She constantly popped over unannounced, and then I had to
take her to court to get my deposit returned. With the housing issue in
the city settled I drove my family to suburban Overland Park, Kansas.

My tenure as assistant to Dean Demopoulos lasted only 11 months,
the length of time he coached at UMKC before moving on. Demopoulos
spent almost 20 years at Temple University with John Chaney. Now he
was gone after one season. I must have that type of effect on people.

Demopoulos and I had walked into a firestorm at UMKC. The
athletics director, Bob Thomas, fired Bob Sundvold, the previous
coach, who recorded the most wins (16) in his four-year tenure. When
questioned on the move, Thomas refused to discuss details publicly.
That meant Demopoulos came in with the task of building bridges
with the players, the community and the media. Knowing who you can
trust is extremely important in the coaching profession. Every move is
scrutinized by the media; therefore, you don't want any disloyal people in
your inner circle. No coach likes to pick up the newspaper and read what
is said in a private meeting, so we stuck to the business of trying to put
the best team on the floor.

As a Chaney disciple, Demopoulos stressed two of Chaney's basketball beliefs. On offense it was about avoiding turnovers. "Don't give your enemy extra bullets to shoot at you" was a common saying for Demopoulos. On defense it was about installing the Temple zone philosophy. He was successful on both fronts. We finished the year ranked second in the country in fewest turnovers (Temple was first) and No. 1 in the Mid-Continent Conference in fewest points allowed. I learned as much that year as I had in all my previous years combined.

Dean was very driven and focused. But the most important lesson he taught me was patience when dealing with players. That wasn't the easiest thing to do when you start off 0-4 like we did.

Our first game was at Morris Brown University in Atlanta. While the players warmed up on the court, the manager from Morris Brown walked into our locker room where we were sitting and went to a caged area where some equipment was stored. As he started counting the uniforms I saw Dean's face turn red. I hustled the guy out before Demopoulos exploded. All I could say facetiously to him was, "Welcome to the big time." I doubt that ever happened to him while he was at Temple, but it didn't faze me at all. Another story for the book.

His patience paid off as the team got more comfortable with the new system. We went on a four-game winning streak. The biggest Kangaroo win was a double digit road triumph against Nebraska (82-71) at its own tournament in Lincoln. I was sold and so were the players. We wound up with a winning record (9-7) in the Mid-Con. If one of our starters hadn't undergone an emergency appendectomy late in the year, I'm sure we would have had an overall winning record.

When the season ended Dean's phone was busy. He interviewed for the head job at Drexel, then was offered the St. Bonaventure job. I was all set to move to Olean, New York when the Seattle SuperSonics called. That presented a problem.

If a head coach takes another job in college, the assistant has a chance to either become the head coach or accompany him to his new job. If a head coach takes a job in the NBA as an assistant, then the only option is being named the head coach. Otherwise it's another job search. We had a solid first year, but with an overall losing record of 14-16 and fewer wins than Sundvold the previous year. When I took the job, Demopoulos and I had conversations about what would happen if he left, but it unfolded one year too soon. Would the AD be too upset about Dean and want to clean house?

After a weeklong process in which I spoke to the president and board members Thomas decided I was the best option. I'm sure he felt I could provide stability and continuity. Also, in my last year as a head coach at the Division I level, I was named the Coach of the Year in the league.

It happened like this:

The following Monday, Thomas called and wanted to meet me at a restaurant. He didn't want any distractions. At least that's what the optimistic part of me thought. The pessimistic side of me knew I wouldn't make a scene in a public place if I received bad news. As we sat down he wanted to order, but I could care less about food. I wanted to know if I would be packing again. He slid an envelope across the table. Inside the envelope was a contract for the head coaching position. In fact it was the same contract signed by Dean (his name was crossed out). I was offered a four-year deal. My first thought was Colin would not be changing schools again.

It was the shot I had hoped for since I left St. Francis. It was another opportunity to run my own program back at the Division I level.

Smiling faces at the UMKC press conference to announce my appointment. Kids are happy because we won't be moving again.

Granted, it was not Missouri or Kansas, but it was a Division I school.

There are three levels to NCAA Division I basketball, separated by schedules and money in my opinion. Teams at the top, the BCS schools, have the most money and pay teams to play at their place. Some teams like Syracuse or Duke hardly ever play a non-conference road game except on a neutral court. The mid-major teams don't have the money to buy games and also don't need to supplement their budgets with paydays. A payday is playing a game on the road for a guaranteed amount of money. The lowest level is made up of the teams that carry not only their programs, but the athletic departments on their backs for guarantee games as St. Francis, St. Peter's and American University did.

In my first couple of years at UMKC we were funded at the mid to low end of the spectrum. It wasn't until my third year that we began to play two guarantee games each year to help support the athletic department's budget. Through my six years as the Kangaroos head coach we played a total of 15 guaranteed games and brought in more than $500,000. That didn't help my overall record, but helped balance the budget.

Though we hovered around the .500 mark in my first year as the Kangaroos assistant, UMKC was a rebuilding job. The school had only one winning season in the previous eight years, the last year of Sundvold's tenure. The Kangaroos had won only one Mid-Con tournament game in their history. Unlike programs that move up to the Division I level after a successful run at a lower level, UMKC didn't have that tradition to fall back on. We played at three different off-campus arenas—Municipal Auditorium in downtown K.C., Kemper Arena and Hale Arena next door—with no control over our own practice facility. Thank goodness I developed a good working relationship with the woman who ran the building. The other struggle was for exposure because K.C. is a KU town first followed closely by Missouri, then Kansas State. Still, it was my chance to help UMKC carve out a niche.

On the plus side, we had everyone back from a solid team. For only the second time in my career I was able to schedule more home games than road games. Jim Valvano said a long time ago the three keys to winning at the college level were recruiting, scheduling and recruiting. The only other time I had as many home games was in my second year with the UNF Ospreys. At that time I loaded up on northern teams who wanted to make a southern trip. The Ospreys opened with 13 games in a row at home, a longer homestand than the Florida Marlins.

My top assistant, Ken Dempsey, organized the recruiting. I knew Demps for more than 20 years. He had worked at that level his whole career. The players he recruited at Monmouth University and North Carolina-Greensboro helped them qualify for the NCAA tournament. Also, he was the best man in my wedding, so I knew I could always trust him to have my back. I kept Jason Ivey and Jay Byland from the previous staff. They were very good at what they did and, most important, I counted on their loyalty. I know I told myself after Millersville I wouldn't keep someone I don't know from a previous staff, but I felt I knew Ivey and Byland well enough to make that judgement call.

Preseason conditioning was not only a time for guys to get in shape, but also to learn our implemented system. After our morning run we spent time working defensive slides. NCAA rules prohibited the use of a ball, so we used a piece of fruit. We usually worked it through until the apple or orange got too mushy to throw.

Defensively the system was similar to the year before. The players did a good job of grasping the zone concepts. With the addition of a 6-foot-9, 25-year-old junior college player, Tom Curtis, we moved some players around. Out of high school Curtis went straight to work in the construction business. A few years later he decided to become a teacher, so he headed back to school. Curtis is now working in the K.C. school district. His development meant I could play Marcus Golson and Mike Jackson on the wings. They were both 6-foot-8 and long. We were able to cover a lot of ground.

In the back we moved a senior, Matt Suther, from off guard to point. He played it in high school and had a very good feel for the game. Today he is running his own AAU program. Not surprising. Out front we started Mike Watson, a local kid. He was tough and quick, which is what you need at the attack point. That was our starting lineup as we headed into the opening game.

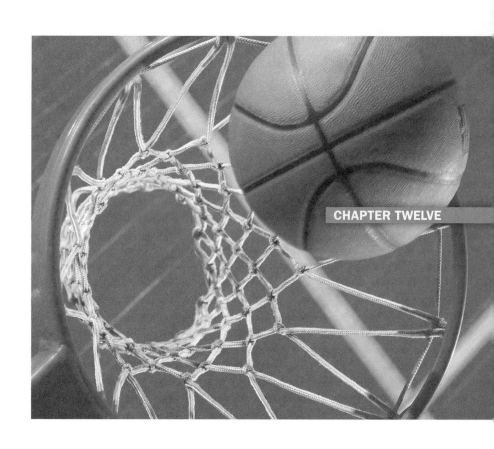

CHAPTER TWELVE

Making the Most of It

O ur opening game of the 2001-02 season was at Wisconsin-Green Bay. The Phoenix continued to be a very good program since the years Dick Bennett coached there. I was a nervous wreck before the game. In my mind I knew we were ready, but in any road game you always must expect the unexpected. Also, I wanted to dispel the notion conveyed by the local media that the only reason I got the job was because I was the players' choice. I wanted to prove the naysayers wrong.

The game started with UWGB making every three-point shot. As we approached the first TV timeout, I re-emphasized to the team that as long as we did not allow them to score in the paint and challenged every shot that the Phoenix could not make enough treys to beat us. A key play late in the game occurred when Mike Jackson was double-teamed, so he whipped a pass to our freshman center, Dan Leadbetter, who caught it and laid it in for a two-point lead. To this day I still don't know how he caught the ball and put it in. Then a three-point basket by Matt Suther gave us a little cushion.

The game came down to the final possession. UWGB's leading scorer missed a three-point shot with Jackson draped all over him. My prophecy was fulfilled. The Phoenix didn't make enough threes to beat us and we snuck out of there with a 48-47 win. After the game we took the players to a neighborhood grill my assistants found. We were able to get steak dinners for less than $7.00. Even after a big win we had to stay within budget. The players didn't seem to mind. Neither did the coaches.

For the moment the only thing that mattered was we were undefeated. I would be wearing my lucky suit for another game, another silly superstition I picked up a few years ago.

We won our next four games to run our record to 5-0. Included in those wins were back-to-back victories over Southwest Missouri State (now Missouri State) and Northern Iowa. Both are out of the Missouri Valley Conference, which arguably has the best mid-major teams in the country. In our fifth game we traveled to Robert Morris College in Pittsburgh. The Colonials were an old rival from my St. Francis days. With about ten minutes to go in the game we were trailing when a timeout was called and the Kangaroos came to the bench. In the huddle I reminded them if we wanted our next game, at Kansas, to have any major significance we needed to beat Robert Morris. So much for the coach's worn out "one game at a time"

Dream up a way to beat Kansas. Came close, but then I woke up.

slogan. I was looking for anything to motivate them. After the timeout, a Robert Morris player stole the ball and dunked on Watson. The wrong thing to do because it served only to spark

Watson. From that moment, Watson took over. He scored 26 points and led us to the win. "Kansas, here we come," I thought.

Though Big 12 teams normally garnered the most fan interest, UMKC was the talk of the town after our start. I sensed that niche we looked to carve out in Kansas City. The 'Roos tied a school Division I record for the longest winning streak (five) with a shot at Goliath. On paper, definitely David vs. Goliath, because KU had three future NBA lottery picks (Drew Gooden, Kirk Hinrich and Nick Collison) in its starting lineup. The only lottery my guys knew was at the local convenience store where lottery tickets were purchased. Both Roy Williams and I had been to the Final Four. As coach, he had taken his teams there; I had taken my sons there as spectators. I bet I had more fun. Kansas had more than 100 years of tradition. We had been at the Division I level for 15 years. You get the picture.

We traveled the night before so our team would be away from campus and the distractions. Kansas was paying us $40,000 for the game, so we figured we'd spend a few dollars. At the game day shootaround I could tell the team was tight. It certainly didn't help when Coach Williams walked into our practice to say hello. I appreciated his hospitality, but when he mistakenly thought my assistant was me I knew I had my pre-game talk. As I related the story to my players they understood the message. It was about respect and making sure at the end of the game the KU fans knew who we were.

The game was close early before the Jayhawks jumped out to a double digit lead. Once again in the second half Mike Watson was unstoppable. They tried Kirk Hinrich, Aaron Miles and Jeff Boschee on him, but it didn't matter. He kept scoring and we closed the gap. With three minutes to go, we had possession trailing by six. After a tough miss by Jackson the Jayhawks finished the game by locking up the win at the free throw line. Our defense had somewhat stymied the Jayhawks. We were one of only seven teams to hold them under 80 points that season in our 79-68 loss. Watson ended up the game's leading scorer with 29.

Our streak was broken, and I could finally send my suit to the cleaners. After seven games (including two exhibitions), my suit could have stood in the corner by itself. The truth is I didn't have a large wardrobe, so a winning streak helped.

During that run we were ranked for the first time in school history in the *USA Today*/ESPN coaches poll and the *College Insider Mid-Major Top 25*. The latter ranking would be as high as 16. We went into Christmas with a 7-2 record. Our only two losses were against No. 4 Kansas and No. 5 Oklahoma State. In the Oklahoma State game, we drew close to 9,000 fans, the second largest crowd ever at Municipal Auditorium.

There was a consistent theme to the rest of the season. Watson was our scoring leader, Jackson our rebounding leader and the other three seniors made plays at the end of tight games to help us win.

A minor scare occurred after our early January game with Texas A&M–Corpus Christi. We anxiously awaited the final grades on two of our freshmen, Ed Spencer and Brandon Lipsey, on the verge of the second semester. Jay Byland received the favorable grades on Lipsey from the registrar before the game, so Lipsey remained eligible for the second semester. I assumed since Byland didn't say anything about Spencer that he was cleared as well. After the game I learned differently. Cynthia Gabel, our compliance officer, told me she did not have any final word on Spencer. Though Spencer played only the last couple minutes in a UMKC blowout victory, we would have been forced to forfeit if his grades came back negative. Upon hearing that I went ballistic on Byland.

Though my tirade was directed toward him, my frustration was about the whole situation. Most schools have an academic advisor for athletics. Since UMKC was in the process of hiring a full-time person for the first time, the responsibility fell on Byland's shoulders. Talk about a conflict of interest.

After my outburst I told Byland I would meet him back at school. Byland drove the players home and was so shook up he sat at a flashing red light for two minutes before Jackson pointed out the light was not going to turn green. Golson, as helpful as he was, told Byland he could have one of his comp tickets for the remaining home games.

Byland and I waited until 8 the next morning when the registrar posted the grades on the computer. In the meantime, I apologized to Byland. He was one of the most conscientious people I had worked with and I knew he felt awful. At 10:08 a.m. the grades were revealed and Spencer remained eligible. We dodged an administrative bullet.

Going into the final weekend of league play we faced our toughest road trip. A Southwest Airlines flight followed by that familiar bus ride from Las Vegas to Cedar City, Utah, made the trip a full-day affair. The first stop was a Thursday night game at Southern Utah followed by a Saturday night game at Chicago State. When we arrived Wednesday afternoon in Vegas, Byland noticed there was no VCR on the bus as we had ordered. Seems someone stole it (New York déjà vu). The three-hour bus ride was our only chance to watch game film, so we decided to eat in Vegas and wait for a new bus. And wait we did. It took three hours to get a new bus. Once we arrived in Cedar City we went straight to the gym for a quick practice. It was 11 p.m. before we finally checked into the hotel. In the first half we played like we were still on the bus.

At halftime I noticed the players staring at a sign in the visitors locker room. SUU conveniently erected a sign about the elevation and the effects of altitude sickness. I knew if I let them give in we were through, so we decided to press from the opening possession in the second half.

I wasn't going to give my team a chance to think about being tired. We gradually cut into the lead and won, 72-71, in overtime. Watson scored 31 points to lead us in scoring while Golson grabbed seven rebounds. So much for the altitude. It only bothers you when you aren't making any shots.

That night we traveled back to Vegas and I let them relax. It was also an opportunity for me to visit with one of my former players, Brian Sitter, who had moved back to Vegas. At midnight Ivey and Dempsey conducted a bed check and started thinking about Chicago State.

The last conference game made me most nervous. It was Chicago State's senior night, and CSU had not won a league game in almost two years. You'd think the odds were certainly in their favor. When you play a team that hasn't won in a long time you feel like they're due. Early in the game things started to get weird.

At one point Suther lost his shoe bringing up the ball. The trailing official picked it up and held onto it. When Suther made the entry pass the official threw his shoe at him. At the same time Suther's teammate threw the ball back. With no desire to be decked by a shoe Suther ducked. As the ball flew toward our bench I saw two Chicago State players ready to grab it with the possibility of an easy lay-up. So I grabbed the ball and held onto it. The official walked over, ready to give me a technical before I reminded him he threw a shoe at my player. Based on that piece of evidence he compromised. He gave them the ball. No technical. It was the only time in my career I convinced an official to change his mind.

Three minutes later a couple of grade school kids, while playing around at the end of the Cougars bench, knocked over the water cooler. The water spilled onto the floor, so the game was stopped until it was cleaned up. Towels didn't work because the water seeped under the floorboards. Then someone tried hair dryers. After a few more minutes, some fans came out of the stands and started to dance on the floor with towels under their feet. As I sat there, I wondered if that ever happened to Bob Knight. At least they didn't try baby powder. Finally, the game resumed and Jackson carried us with 29 points in UMKC's 61-48 victory. One of the strangest wins in my career.

The Mid-Con tournament began with us playing our best basketball since early in the season. The first night we pulled away down the stretch for a 70-57 win over Southern Utah. In the semis we met the conference power, Valparaiso.

Coach Homer Drew directed his program in that stretch to six NCAA tournaments in seven years. They were the gold standard for the league. The Crusaders were the type of program every low or mid-major team aspired to be. During their run of NCAA tournament appearances they had made history by advancing all the way to the Sweet Sixteen in 1998. Every year fans relive Valpo's success when the buzzer beater by Homer's son Bryce is shown on television. It is still regarded as one of the crowning moments in the history of the NCAA tournament.

The team Homer Drew assembled in 2002 was as good as any of his previous teams in the NCAA tournament. The Crusaders had beaten us twice during the year. On the Crusaders floor they had jumped on us early and never let up in a 76-63 victory. On the bus ride to the airport I was so mad we had our film session right there. With the tape rolling and the misplays flashing again before me I became even more incensed and the F-bombs started to fly. I'm not sure what the team got out of my rant, but I sure felt better. They probably did, too, because they knew it was over. One of the most important things I learned about coaching is once you make corrections, it's time to start preparations for the next game.

The conference tournament semifinal game went back and forth, but in the end Valpo's depth wore us down. The Crusaders started a bigger front line than most NBA teams. They even brought a seven-footer off the bench. Valparaiso was one of the first teams to take advantage of using older foreign players. Three of their five starters hailed from outside the United States and had the experience of playing in a foreign professional league. The rules have since been tightened to eliminate some of the foreign players, but the new rules didn't help us that night. We ended the season with the most Division I wins (18) in school history and advanced to the conference tournament semis for only the second time.

Following a successful season at most schools, the budget is increased or facilities are improved. At UMKC we went in the other direction. I was informed in the spring of 2002 if I wanted my players to attend summer school, I would have to raise the money. Just when I thought I was out of the fundraising business.

To pay for the players' summer school, I needed to come up with some money quickly. Through the generosity of Jay Byland's mother Liz, we had four Richard Petty Driving experiences to auction. My next call was to Kevin Carter at NFL Merchandise. He played for me at Loyola and later became a vice president with NFL Merchandise. Carter forwarded me an autographed Joe Montana helmet, Troy Aikman jersey and Joe Namath football. The last piece of the puzzle was Tubby Smith obliging my request for an autographed basketball. I felt like I was on a scavenger hunt. All my contacts came through and we raised enough money for the players to attend summer school. I hit paydirt the following summer when a longtime season ticket holder agreed to donate $150,000 to cover summer school. That took me out of the fundraising business for a couple of years.

With five seniors graduating the question was, "Can UMKC continue the momentum?" The early season answer was a resounding "No!" At Christmas time we were 1-7. A year after receiving votes for the top 25, we were trying to figure out how to win a game. The toughest thing for a school like UMKC is consistency, which results from a pool of talented players growing in the system. As a commuter school with little basketball tradition, it was amazing how many firsts were accomplished in 2002. Then in 2002-03, we were off to the worst start in school history. The year before we were only six points down to KU with three minutes left in the game. In 2002-03, I would have been happy to be only six touchdowns behind with three minutes left. The only player with experience was Watson.

Enjoying a great start to his junior year, Watson had a supporting cast that was too young. He was one of the leading scorers in the country and almost single-handedly beat Colorado. He scored 36 points, but he had to be removed in the final minute because of severe leg cramps. At that point I was desperate to try anything.

In the midst our annual New Year's Eve camp, I made a decision that changed our season. One of my student assistants was a former player by the name of Marc Stricker. He gave up his last year of competition because of multiple knee operations. He wanted to enter coaching, so I kept him on as an assistant. Life does come full circle. Coach Hohenberger would have been proud of me.

What the team really needed was another experienced guard to take the load off Watson. At the camp we discussed his ability to come back. For it to happen, I had to clear it with our Gabel, our compliance officer. Since Marc had a year of eligibility left and we weren't using our 13th scholarship, he was cleared to play. His first game was our first league game at Chicago State.

The night before the game I met with my former assistant John Rhodes, who was then at Ohio University. OU was in Chicago to play DePaul. When our conversation drifted to players, I mentioned Watson's cramping problem. He suggested pickle juice. At first I thought he was kidding, but I saw he was serious. The next day I sent my assistant to the grocery store for a jar of pickles. For the next two years Watson drank a jar of pickle juice before every game and never cramped up again.

Eight minutes into the Chicago State game, Stricker picked up three fouls. It looked like my idea was going to be a bust. However, in the second half Stricker came through with two big threes and some clutch free throws down the stretch. We walked out of there with a win, 80-70, and a good start in league play. Two nights later at Southern Utah we missed on the final possession and lost, 82-78.

The team seemed to gain a tremendous amount of confidence from that opening trip. We went on to win seven of the last 11 games including another first-round win in the conference tournament, 76-73, over Oral Roberts. Two games stood out along with an off-the-court development.

The day before we left for Western Illinois, the athletics director gave me a two-year extension. I was very excited about his confidence and saw it as a sign we were heading in the right direction. With a new extension, the team took off on a four-game winning streak, including an overtime win, 71-68, at Valparaiso. It was the first time UMKC ever won at Valparaiso and only the third victory overall against the Crusaders in school history.

After the game I phoned Metro Sports general manager John Denison, who was instrumental in putting together our TV package. He chose to broadcast every road game at Valparaiso, but that was the first year he didn't make the trip because of surgery to remove kidney stones.

I heard the excitement in his voice and it was a great feeling to hear the enthusiasm from someone who waited so long. After hanging up I told TV analyst Neil Harwell that Denison would not be allowed to make the trip to Valparaiso again until we lost. Superstition is superstition. You can't mess with the basketball gods.

The other game that stood out was the night the Mike Watson scored 54 points in a double overtime win at Oral Roberts. After they beat us earlier in the year by 14, I was hoping for a better showing the next time around against ORU. As I looked to the end of the court I saw the posted slogan, "Expect a Miracle." We definitely needed one that night. Watson started off slowly but had the ability to score in bunches. By the second half he was in a zone. Seemed every shot thrown up went in.

One time he stepped between two defenders and knocked down a three-point shot. Down the stretch he refused to let us lose. His line read 19 of 35 from the floor, 10 of 22 from the three-point line and 6 of 6 from the foul line. An unbelievable performance. Thank goodness he drank his pickle juice. And another record was set that night: Marc Stricker became the first player in NCAA history to play 50 minutes without scoring a point. Somebody had to pass the ball to Watson.

When the season ended we hit the recruiting trail for what was our most important recruiting year in my tenure at UMKC. It meant spending more time in the car. It was not uncommon to drive five or six hours one-way to evaluate and talk with a player. To save money I got in the car and drove straight back. There were plenty of strange looks from coaches when I told them I was driving back the same day. Ken Dempsey accompanied me on many of the trips. It was an airport trip, however, that almost got assistants Dempsey and Byland fired.

It was an afternoon game at Oakland University outside Detroit, so I planned to fly to Tucson afterward to see a junior college game. Byland felt confident he had the quickest route to the airport after relaying it to me from an assistant at OU. After the game, I took a few minutes to talk with my parents, a former player, and couple of high school teammates who had seen the game. I had no idea about the adventure that lied ahead.

The first traffic jam wasn't too bad. But the next one put us at a standstill. It seems the road was closed due to construction, so all traffic was diverted. My temperature increased as we moved not an inch. Feeling the trip slip away, I yelled for Demps to circumvent the traffic by driving on the berm. He looked at me like I was crazy. At that point I got out of the car and walked. Where, I had no idea. It was about 30 degrees in February, so the cold air hit me right away. When I got back into the car he still didn't understand what a berm was. I guess I didn't explain myself very well. It was clear I wasn't going to make the flight to Tucson, so the next hope was making the team return flight to Kansas City. We arrived in barely enough time to board. When I sat down next to Byland he tried to explain, but I was in no mood to listen. Then when Jackson offered Byland his seat, I don't think I ever saw Byland move so quickly. My players seemed to always be helpful toward Byland at his most tenuous moments. To this day Demps still does not know what a berm is.

The rest of our recruiting went well. We landed a point guard, Brandon Temple, who had signed the previous year but finally graduated from junior college. He played high school basketball for a former player of mine in North Carolina. He flunked math three times and didn't graduate on time from Missouri State University-West Plains, a junior college in southern Missouri. If we had him the previous year I'm convinced we would have won a few more games. But I made a commitment to him so I kept a scholarship open for him. Temple repaid my loyalty with two very good seasons and, most important, a bachelor's degree from UMKC.

UMKC also beat out the University of Maine for Mike English, a 6-foot-4 forward out of Kaskaskia (Ill.) Community College, who became an all-conference player for the 'Roos. He received his GED in St. Louis before attending junior college. He was a smart kid who missed too many high school classes to graduate on time. Maine had him convinced he could graduate in their mechanical engineering program. Knowing his math and science grades, I was not as easily convinced. Because he liked to work on cars doesn't automatically make him an engineer. He was similar to one of my recruits at St. Francis who wanted to major in engineering, but when pressed on what he wanted to do, replied he wanted to drive the subway train. I had two choices with Mike. At the risk of losing him I could be honest, or I could con him like the coach at Maine tried to do. I chose honesty. Two years later Mike not only finished up a great career, but also received a Bachelor of Arts degree with an emphasis in communications.

One of the other high school players we signed, Jeremiah Hartsock, was a Mormon out of Bartlesville, Oklahoma. I had never recruited a Mormon before, so that was a new experience. A key to recruiting a player is learning his background and what makes him tick. In researching all the literature I could on the Church of the Latter Day Saints, I found out the church has a huge base in Independence, Missouri, and I knew I was in business. Please don't confuse me with Nick Nolte in *Blue Chips*, the movie in which the main character changed his religion as often as people change their underwear. I understood the significance of a Mormon player on my team. He was with us for a year, then went on his church mission in Russia. He was 6-foot-9 so I guess it was a pretty good tradeoff. At the low to mid-major level you have to use any advantage or connection you have.

Another player signed through a connection was Brent Stephens. One day in my office, I got a phone call from former KU coach Ted Owens. I met him when he was the athletics director at St. Leo College in Florida. He told me about a player who left Monmouth University to return to his hometown of Jay, Oklahoma. Stephens was a raw boned kid who wanted more playing time while playing closer to home. Thanks to my friendship with Coach Owens, he became a Kangaroo. I always believed you should be in the office early and stay late because you never knew when someone would call about a good player. It took me 20 years to have my theory pay off.

Sometimes in recruiting you need to go great distances. Based on a recommendation of a friend coaching in New Zealand I decided to recruit Alex Pledger, a seven-footer from Hamilton, New Zealand. When I finally got approval from Thomas to travel there I had to make sure I got him.

That spring I boarded a plane to Los Angeles, then caught a connecting flight to New Zealand. Though I had been to Warsaw, Poland, to evaluate players at a camp, the trip to New Zealand was my first time overseas to make a home visit. Before I landed in Auckland I was in the air for 16 hours. I rented a car without any problems (I had my driver's license and credit card that time) and drove to Hamilton. It was only a 90-minute drive, but difficult to get used to driving on the opposite side of the road. Thank goodness it was a busy day and I stayed on the left side where I was supposed to be. I met with Alex and his parents and it went well until I realized my plug on my laptop would not work in their outlet. Before the trip I spent two weeks putting together a power point presentation on the computer and felt very proud about the way it turned out. Now, I thought, it was all for naught. His brother luckily played a lot of video games and had a converter. With that problem settled we had a good visit.

When the visit ended I got in the car and drove back to Auckland. The only sights seen were dairy cows on the side of the road. The next morning I boarded a plane for home. Another 16 hours in the air and I was back in Kansas City after only 48 hours in New Zealand. I had to laugh when Sandy asked me what the country looked like. I could only describe to her the roadside dairy cows, the appearance of the gym and his house.

The other recruit we signed that year was my next door neighbor. One day Sandy stood in the driveway when Brian Gettinger's mother saw her and stopped to talk. She told Sandy her son was a good basketball player. Sandy had heard it all before many times, but the only thing different that time was the last line. He was 6-foot-9. Usually the story ended by the parent saying their son was 5-foot-9. Sandy gave me the heads up and we signed him in the fall. For that recruit it took me three minutes to walk to his house.

That summer another connection paid off. Mike Watson, a rising senior, got a shot to play in the Superior League in Puerto Rico. During our bus ride to Oakland University from Indianapolis in his junior season, we started talking about his future and how he could improve his game. When he talked about playing professionally I told him there are a lot of places to make money playing basketball. I related to him how one of my former players, Ricky Melendez, played a dozen years in Puerto Rico. Watson blurted out he was part Hispanic. He said his great grandmother was born there, something to do with his great-great grandfather being stationed there. I told him if he could prove it I was sure we could find a team for him.

As unbelievable as it sounds, Watson could play in the league and get paid without losing his eligibility. It was a loophole in the NCAA rules. The league claimed that they were preparing Puerto Rican players for the Olympics. I think it was a case of someone knowing the right people to get the exemption approved. Players and coaches have been working in the Superior League for as long as I can remember.

When we got back from the trip he sat down with Byland and myself to explain the connection. That was the easy part. The tough part was documenting it. We needed birth certificates for everyone from his great grandmother down. His mother and Mike were easy. The others proved to be more challenging.

The closest military base with archives was Fort Riley, Kansas, about three hours away. Without hesitation Byland drove to the army base. To this day I can't believe how many hours and days he spent researching and finding the right documents. In the end he did it. We had the documentation.

Now I had to find a team and a contract. We found Watson a team, the Carolina Gigantes. They were coached by former Marquette great Butch Lee, another Puerto Rican national. Five years later Watson is still making good money in the summer playing in the Superior League. The first year he brought me back a team shirt, one of the best gifts I ever received.

Turning 40 and experiencing a losing season raised the question of how much time I had left. I contemplated jumping out of an airplane or running a marathon as a way to show Father Time I wasn't quite through yet. Sandy convinced me the marathon would be safer, but at the 20-mile mark I didn't agree with her.

That spring I trained for the Chicago Marathon. I quickly got a true appreciation for the type of effort and training a runner endures. When I finally finished my last long run (20 miles) I knew there was no turning back. Frankly, I overtrained and my legs were killing me. But word leaked out to the newspapers, so I had no alternative but to push ahead.

With six miles left I hit the wall. I knew I should have taken the parachute jump instead. Actually, I think I hit the wall six miles into the marathon. I finished in just slightly more than four hours. Then I had two hours to catch my plane home. I made the plane, but the flight attendant had to pry me out of my seat when we landed in Kansas City.

Following the marathon we had a winning season in 2003-04. With no desire to upset the basketball gods I continued to run a marathon in each of the next three years. I ended up running in five, but my marathon career ended after a losing season. I think I jinxed myself by running two before the 2006-07 season.

Stalking the sidelines at the Mid Continent Conference Tournament.

The next two years proved to be a roller coaster ride on and off the court. We opened up the 2003-04 season with a loss to Minnesota in the pre-season NIT, a defeat to this day I blame on Coach K at Duke. The Minnesota Gophers had a freshman by the name of Kris Humphries who signed with Duke. Coach K wanted him in Durham the summer before his freshman year, but Humphries did not want to go until the fall. After three national championships, a coach can make those demands. If not met, a high school All-American is discarded without a second thought. So Humphries ended up with the Golden Gophers.

Humphries was one of the first cases where a player got out of his letter of intent without any penalties. Because of that case the floodgates opened. It even helped us the following year, but on that night it killed us. He played like a pro he later became and dropped a double-double on us. I always wondered if a player leaving UMKC would be treated the same. I doubt it.

December 30, 2003, and March 8, 2004, are two dates that forever stick in my mind. Both had a great bearing on coaches losing their jobs. The first date was the night of UMKC's game with Kansas State. The second was the semifinal game of the Mid-Con tournament.

Going into our home game with K-State, we had a hard time stopping opponents from scoring. We played more man-to-man, but it wasn't working. We lost on the road to Youngstown State, 73-65, a team we should have beaten. I decided to spend the following week working on the zone defenses that were so good to us the first year.

When we opened the game in a zone, it was clear K-State had only prepared for a man-to-man defense. If the Wildcats had watched tapes of the previous games, that's all they would have seen. We were up by 18 at halftime. Though there were almost 8,000 fans in the arena, the fourth largest crowd in UMKC history, it was as quiet as a church. Most of them wore K-State purple, so the Wildcats definitely had more fans that night even though it was a home gam. I wish I could claim credit for the home game, but it was the end of a contract signed three years before I arrived. The game had been pushed back for three years. I think they were waiting for Mike Jackson to graduate, but that's only my speculation.

The final score ended up 93-52. It was the fifth largest margin of victory in Kangaroo history and the first time we ever beat K-State. Quite honestly, the score could have been worse. With five minutes to go we started taking the air out of the ball, trying not to show anyone up, and preventing us from blowing the lead. At one point I turned to Demps and told him there were only 15 more possessions left in the game and based on my math I thought we were okay. Looking at me, he told me to sit down and clear the bench. I did and relaxed for the moment.

The next day I was interviewed by ESPN about the win. It was great. On the other side the talking heads on TV and radio surmised that Jim Wooldridge would lose his job because of that loss. Wooldridge, however, was given a reprieve at the end of the year. The next season he was let go unceremoniously on his way to the locker room after a loss in the Big 12 Tournament. Another AD (Tim Weiser) who failed to display some professionalism. When I saw Bob Huggins, who replaced Wooldridge a year later, Huggins confirmed that the loss to UMKC was a major factor in his dismissal. In response to my desire to continue the series, Huggins told me KSU would never come back to K.C.

Signaling to slow down to hold the score down vs. Kansas State.

to play since Weiser had told him he decided to fire Wooldridge after the Wildcats loss to us. Why Weiser waited another full season, I don't know.

Three nights later on the same court we lost our league opener to Oral Roberts, 91-71. So much for the momentum gained by a monumental win. Kids will be kids no matter how much you try to keep them on an even keel. As Demopoulos used to say, "They started smelling themselves."

On March 8th we played the game that could have changed history for the UMKC program. A team that wins the conference tournament becomes synonymous with success. It gets you on television and in the NCAA tournament. For most mid-major programs, those moments are fleeting. As a coach it gets you a new contract or a bigger job. Make the most of it and you wear the brass ring. If you don't, you wear a crown of thorns.

We faced our nemesis, Valparaiso, for the third straight year in the semifinal game. That time it was in front of 5,000 home fans. The game started out looking like the night UMKC would make school history. We were playing our best basketball. Going into the game we won six of our final nine games. In the first round we defeated Oral Roberts by 13. Against Valpo we were up 17 points in the first half and Kemper Arena was rocking. After a timeout Valpo scored back-to-back three-point goals, both by Greg Tonagel off the bench. Similar to what we did the previous year when we brought back Stricker, the Crusaders activated sixth-year senior Tonagel at mid-year. He proved to be a stabilizing force.

With ten seconds to go in the first half, up by ten, an official made a momentum-changing call. Through the years I have seen calls go both ways. Not that I am a coach who believes it evens out. I am still waiting on that one. An over-the-back call was made on a tip slam rebound by Mike English. It was his second foul, which at the time seemed unimportant, but the replay clearly shows the only player near him was Corey Starks, one of English's teammates. The play was so amazing it was shown on ESPN's Play of the Day. I say that not to brag, but to share how depressing it was to see a play that may have cost my season and my next job over and over and over again on national TV. To add further insult, the basket was nullified. Instead of going into the locker room with a double digit lead and sky high confidence, UMKC's halftime margin was eight.

Three minutes into the second half English picked up his third and fourth fouls. For all intents and purposes he was done for the night. We tried to hang on without him, but in the end Valpo's depth wore us down. They went on to win the conference tournament, and I went back to the drawing board.

The next day I was drilled in the paper for blowing the lead. I can live with being criticized, but not one reporter got it right. The question should have been why English was still in the game with three fouls early in the second half. As former Michigan State standout Scott Skiles once said, "Basketball is like church. Many attend, but few understand."

CHAPTER THIRTEEN

The Big Marsupial

Carlton Aaron was a 6-foot-9 senior, listed at 300 pounds. He was closer to 330. The only reason he looked thinner as a senior was because we got him bigger shorts (5XL). He transferred from Temple after his freshman year, the first recruit I met and signed at UMKC. He had a big heart and a big appetite to go with it.

Everyone seemed to be amazed by his size. It was always interesting to see how people reacted to the "Big Marsupial" (a nickname given to him by a local radio station.). Normally he handled jokes about his size very well, but on one occasion he didn't.

During a pregame meal at Centenary, one of his teammates ribbed him about his weight. He resisted hitting him and instead turned and punched a hole in the wall. I was ready to give the owner my credit card to pay for the damage, but instead the owner asked Aaron to sign the wall. Then he took a picture of Aaron and his daughter in front of the hole. I guess he was starting some sort of wall of fame and Aaron was the first inductee.

Three years before, Coach Dempsey and I had gone to see him and his mother in the Bronx to seal the deal. I told Demps to find a parking spot while I went inside. An hour later he was still looking for a spot.

I love New York! Carlton, his mother and I talked about how different it would be at UMKC. I swore that I would help him accomplish two things—become a good player and get a degree. It took two-and-a-half years for him to reach his potential and it was a constant battle to keep his weight in check. I went by his house every week to confiscate any stashed Ring Dings or Twinkies. I could feed my entire family for a month on some of my food raids I made at Aaron's house.

One summer he went home and swore he wouldn't go to the pizza place or Chinese restaurant across the street from his house. I still remember his mom saying she was going to bake his chicken. Two weeks later he came back 22 pounds heavier. She must have been baking more than chicken.

Each year he would quit and each year I talked him out of it. The first year I talked him out of it was over a late night Frosty from Wendy's. I made him buy his own so I wouldn't break NCAA rules. What a joke! In his senior year I got a call from his mother telling me he was quitting. She said I had beaten down his morale and she thought it was okay if he quit. That was after a 31-point performance against Centenary. When I called Demps, he said not to worry.

We had a couple of extra days to find him, so I searched. Since he wasn't at his apartment, I went to where I was led to believe he'd be working. It was a place called The Shady Lady (a gentleman's club). I sent my assistant in to check while I sat in the car. The last thing I needed was someone seeing me in there. He wasn't there. Finally, I found him at the Steak n Shake. I should have known. After I told him he owed it to his mother to finish the season and graduate he came to his senses. He was named all-conference and graduated in the spring.

That summer his mother threw a graduation/going-away party for him before he left to play professionally in England. Mrs. Aaron made sure Demps and I were there before she toasted the occasion. Her toast was one of the best moments of my coaching career. She quoted scriptures in talking about the rams and sheep, then thanked me for everything I did for her son. It was not easy for her to admit that I knew what was best for her son since there had been many times we were on opposite sides of the fence. To this day I am still trying to figure out if I were a ram or a sheep, but it doesn't matter. The only thing that matters is that her son is a college graduate on his way to a successful life.

CHAPTER FOURTEEN

The Lucky Buckeye
and the Streak

Being from Ohio, one knows that a buckeye is a good luck charm. It you're from outside Ohio you might think it's a worthless nut. That worthless nut provided some of the best luck of my career and a special moment between father and son.

My fourth season as head coach at UMKC was one of the most memorable of my career. On New Year's Eve that year, however, I would have told you differently.

I suspended two starters for missing a film session after we returned from Colorado. The decision was monumental because we were winless (0-6) and our next game was on the road against Wichita State. I must have been crazy. The truth is I had to do something dramatic, so we went to Wichita without Brandon Temple and Mike English. I left them home to decide how they wanted to remember their senior season. Both were good kids at heart, but acting too immature. Soap opera type stuff with their teammates is what I call it.

At halftime we were down by double digits. I was so upset with my team's play I ripped off my shirt in the locker room. Buttons flew everywhere. One stuck on the shoulder of Jeremiah Hartsock, but he didn't move. I wish I could say we came out of the locker room and won the game, but we didn't. However, we did play much better, especially our center Carlton Aaron, who scored 18 and pulled down nine rebounds. It was the breakthrough game we anticipated for two years.

The only other time I did something like that was at Millersville. The difference was it was premeditated at Millersville. In a game at Cheney University (Pa.) that determined whether or not we made the conference tournament. I wrote a big W on my chest with a marker before the players came to the locker room. When I started my pre-game talk about being a warrior I ripped open my shirt for effect. I'm happy to say we came away with a victory in that game. Unlike at UMKC I planned ahead and had a spare shirt. The only thing I didn't plan was not being to wash the W off my chest for a couple weeks. It was worth it for the win though.

We left for Indianapolis on New Year's Day without winning a game in 2004. Our first league game was against IUPUI, which stands for Indiana University-Purdue University-Indianapolis (commonly called 'ooie-pooie'). After reviewing game tapes of IUPUI, I decided to change to a man-to-man defense. They ran a lot of ball screens, but I felt Temple's ability to guard the ball and the anticipation skills of our other starting guard Quinton Day would allow us to neutralize their top two scorers. Another decision I'll always remember.

While sitting in the hotel room the day of the game with my parents, I asked my father to join us on the bus and in the locker room. In all the years of coaching I never did that before. I'm not sure why I did it then. Maybe because I was at rock bottom, or I was looking for some positive karma. Whatever the reason it turned out to be the best thing I ever did.

We won the game by 16, our first win of the season. Two nights later we played at home, and I wanted my father to be there. Sitting in his hotel room after the IUPUI game I told him I had a plane ticket for him to come Saturday. He came and we won again. That time by ten. Next we were on our way to Louisiana to play Centenary. I told him to call mom and tell her I was taking him to Shreveport. The tone of the conversation was a little different than expected. After more than 50 years of marriage they had not been apart for many days at a time, so it took some serious salesmanship. I laughed while hearing my dad beg my mother to let him travel with the team. I promised her I wouldn't let him go to the casino boats. Finally, she relented.

After the 70-66 win at Centenary we played two nights later at home. I refused to book him a ticket back to Cleveland until after that home game against North Dakota State. I decided to have him address the team if we won. As fate would have it, we won our fourth in a row, 80-67. As I turned the team over to him I fully expected a Knute Rockne-type speech. I knew he had it in him as a former coach.

He looked at the team and offered this final thought: "I have brought you this far, the rest is up to you. But I will leave you my lucky buckeye." As he pulled it out of his pocket the place erupted. It was one of the best feelings in my life.

Winning may not solve all problems, but it sure helps. While we were in the midst of that four-game run, Stricker, who became an assistant coach after his playing career with the 'Roos, quit over a philosophical disagreement. My AD approached me with an article in the school newspaper by a writer who wanted me fired. On top of all that, a mother came to see me about her son's lack of playing time. When you're winning it is a lot easier to deal with those problems.

In fact we did not lose the entire month of January. As our win streak reached 11 we were noticed nationally. ESPN bracketologist Joe Lunardi had us included in his NCAA bracket. Once again we were ranked in the mid-major poll.

It took an unbelievable string of events during the final seconds of our game with Chicago State to end the streak. We were up five with 13 seconds. They scored on a drive as we fouled trying block the shot. That cut the lead to three. CSU missed the free throw and Temple fell while rebounding the ball. Traveling. CSU missed the ensuing three-point attempt and one of the Cougar players grabbed the offensive rebound. We covered him as he was trapped in the corner. He threw up a Hail Mary shot with less than two seconds left after switching his pivot foot three times. The tape shows traveling. The official who blew the call was suspended, but a lot of good it did for our team. The shot went in. The Cougars then stole the inbound pass and hit a three-quarter court shot at the buzzer. An amazing streak came to an amazing end. If I tried to sell the script to Hollywood, no chance would anyone buy it. Ironically, the night before our first win I took the team to see the "Flight of the Phoenix." Now one month later we were playing like the Phoenix that rose from the ashes.

We ended the season with four league games in seven days. Because of a scheduling conflict with the ESPN bracketbusters event, we had to switch our Oral Roberts game date. ORU played in the event, yet we were penalized. I doubt any team in any league ever played that type of conference schedule. I challenge you to look it up.

The first game was a rematch with ORU for first place. We beat ORU in Tulsa for the third straight year and had a chance to put ourselves in the driver's seat. The rematch was the best atmosphere for a home game in my four years as the 'Roos head coach. Showing up to the game with their faces painted, the students screamed their heads off. It was like playing a game at Indiana or Duke. In front of more than 7,000 we won to take over sole possession of first place. Our excitement was tempered by the fact that we had our toughest road trip beginning the next day.

We flew to Chicago State for a chance at revenge. The game was close the whole way, but another bizarre blown official's call was instrumental in the outcome. With the score tied and less than a minute to play, Quinton Day poked the ball free and had one man to beat. At half court the defender poked at the ball, clearly fouling him as the ball came loose. The official raised his arm and gave a toot to his whistle. It was a short sound and he tried to call it back. Our players stopped as Chicago State picked up the ball to go in for a layup. Fortunately, the trailing official blew his whistle to stop the action. The officials huddled to discuss it. I thought we were okay because, if it were ruled an inadvertent whistle, the possession arrow rested in our favor.

After the discussion, the official who blew his whistle, Gene Monge, said the ball came free before he blew it. With no recourse at my disposal, Chicago State got the ball and scored. We would end up losing the game at the buzzer, 74-72. Afterward I pleaded my case with the supervisor of officials. Actually, I pounded on the table and screamed that he cost us a title and a contract extension for me. I ended up eventually being right on both accounts. I must have argued longer than I thought because Mark Onweller, a former college teammate who attended the game, went home before I could talk with him. Probably for the best. I wouldn't have been very good company.

When we watched the tape, it was clear Monge blew the call. It was the last game he officiated in our league. One game too many if you ask me.

We flew to Southern Utah knowing we had to win. That time the altitude combined with the fatigue of playing our third game played in five days got us. We wore out at the end and lost by five. It was 3 in the morning by the time we got back to Vegas. We had a noon flight to Kansas City, so the team could sleep a couple of extra hours. When we arrived at the airport we found out our flight was delayed because of mechanical problems. I am all for fixing it while it's on the ground, but when we were about to board we were delayed again. An elderly woman died on the plane, so we had to wait for the paramedics to remove the body. That was not a good omen. When we finally got back to K.C., it was 9 p.m. Instead of holding practice I sent the team home and headed for the office.

With a number of Monday games that year we often practiced Sunday night. Usually, it was after playing Saturday. We called them our Popeye practices, so named because we fed the players Popeyes chicken after practice. The players seemed to like it because they saved on their monthly meal allotment. They received $800 a month to cover the cost of room and board, more than $100 less than the NCAA allotted. Our budget did not support the full amount. It was another way to help our players and another example of the coaches being the buffer between perception and reality.

The fourth and last game of the week was our senior night against Valparaiso. I knew we would be tired, but I was hoping the crowd would pump us up. Almost 5,000 fans turned out to encourage us. That year turned out to be the best attendance year in school history. We had crowds in the neighborhood of 5,000-7,000 people every night since the beginning of the year. And unlike in the past, they came to see us, not our opponent.

I was proud of how we fought that night. We trailed almost the whole game and by five (78-73) with a minute to go. A three-point shot by Brandon Temple with seven seconds left in the game gave us the win, the only time we enjoyed a lead the whole night. It was a great way for the seniors to go out. After the game the players signed autographs for more than an hour. The downside of the night was ORU capturing the league title by one game. (I wish I could get one of those Chicago State games back.) The other downer was the AD scolding me in the locker room for allowing the players to sign their shoes and give them to young kids in the crowd. Thomas ripped me saying my players shouldn't be giving away their shoes when the track team couldn't afford to buy shoes for their runners. I guess that is why I am not an administrator. However, I wasn't going to let him ruin my joy that night.

The media outpouring for that team was incredible. All *The Kansas City Star* newspaper columnists wrote articles on the team. Television stations wanted to interview players after practice. I felt like I was at Missouri instead of Missouri-Kansas City. It was an exciting time to be a Kangaroo. We even had a resolution set forth on the floor of the state house. I guess it was a slow day and a chance for the local state representative to get a photo op. I was happy to do it because that state rep was our former team manager for two years. He told me it was much easier to deal with college basketball players than his fellow politicians. When our bus departed for the conference tournament in Tulsa all the television stations showed up to send us off. That was a first!

On the bus ride the air conditioner broke. For some reason the bus driver tried to fix it by turning on the heater. That only made it worse. By the time we got to the hotel everyone was sweating so much they only had shorts on. I should have known that was a bad sign.

It is funny how one game can change your season. If we had won either of the Chicago State games we would have been the No. 1 seed and matched against Southern Utah. Instead we were up against the underachieving Oakland Grizzlies. Not a good matchup for us. Led by future NBA player Rawle Marshall, the Grizzlies upset us in the first round. A great season came to a bitter end.

Though our season ended on a sour note, I was rewarded for my team's efforts by being named Mid-Continent Conference Coach of the Year. Also, I was named the *CBS Sportsline* and *College Insider* Coach of the Year. As conference coach of the year in 2005, I became one of only 35 active coaches to be named coach of the year in two different conferences while coaching at two separate schools. I would have traded all of the honors for a chance to cut down the nets with a berth to the NCAA tournament.

My last two years at UMKC were a study of how injuries and the NCAA affect programs at the low major level. I helplessly watched as my best post player broke his hand and missed the first ten games. The following year an all-league post player tore his ACL. The BCS schools have more depth and therefore a better chance to overcome injuries. However, at the low major level, adjusting is more of a challenge. I'm not making excuses, just stating facts.

Corner office with a window. Notice the bowl of fruit on the desk to feed my players anytime they stopped by. Guess I broke an NCAA rule?

We overcame the first injury with our third straight winning regular season and a third place finish in the Mid-Con. Not bad for a team that lost three senior all-conference players from the year before. Unfortunately, we lost in the opening round of the conference tournament. The first question after the game from our beat writer was, "Do you think your job is safe?" Over four years UMKC had the second most conference wins. However, for the second straight year, we had lost in the first round of the tournament. If I were at KU, I could understand that question. But I rebuilt a program that experienced only one winning season in the eight years prior to my tenure. I sure wish I had a snappy comeback. The reality was we started to raise expectation levels. I wish the budget had been raised as well.

Because of budget cuts we lost funding for our managers and one staff person. Then our director of basketball operations was split with the women's team. That resulted in some interesting situations at practice and on the road.

At practice during the last couple of seasons, we had to adjust each plan by the number of coaches available. At one practice we were really short on staff. One assistant was on the road recruiting, and the operations guy was cutting tape for the women's team. I wanted to open practice with a defensive transition drill, but to do that I needed a coach at each end and someone to run the clock.

We were one person short. Or were we? The assistant from Northwestern, Paul Lee, stopped by to watch practice while he was in town recruiting. He had planned on watching, but I put him to work. Fortunately, he graduated from Columbia so he was well-equipped to run the clock. Thanks Paul for the help! The following year we had a player break his foot the first day of practice. We had our new timekeeper!

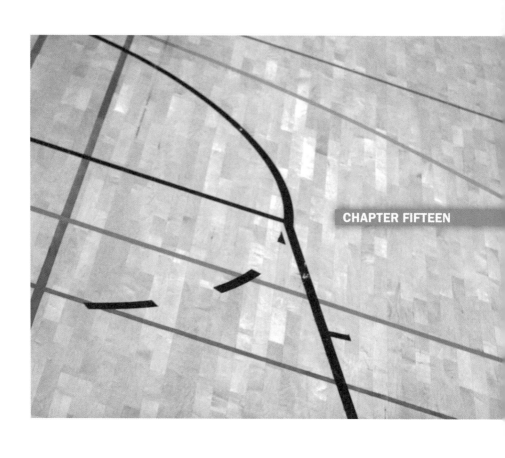

CHAPTER FIFTEEN

NCAA Rules Make No Sense

T he NCAA has become more lenient when granting waivers, but you must sell it. Kalu Guasco was a junior college transfer from Brazil. When we recruited him we knew we would have to appeal for another year. Our compliance officer, who spent a number of years working at the NCAA office, thought we could win the appeal.

Guasco was a straight-A engineering student, but had been in junior college for three-and-a-half years. He enrolled in the junior college in January the first year, then redshirted the following year to learn English. When he came to this country he did not speak English at all. You wouldn't know speaking to him today. Guasco's junior college coach told him the extra year would not hurt him. The coach did that to keep Guasco playing for him one more year because the coach knew Guasco would give him a chance to win more games. Not knowing any better, Guasco stayed. Unfortunately the NCAA said he should have known better. How about that? He listened to his coach, who deliberately gave him bad information and the NCAA said it didn't matter. That is ridiculous. Guasco was a foreign player with no family to advise him, and his only "assistance" was provided by a coach who deliberately lied to him. I can't think of a better case where the NCAA could look after the welfare of a player first and foremost. If UMKC had been a BCS program I believe there's no doubt Guasco would have been granted another year of eligibility.

Once he got to UMKC our compliance officer changed her tune and didn't think we could win the appeal. In the end she talked to the league office and didn't file a full appeal with the NCAA. When I disagreed, she said there was nothing I could do. I felt sick to my stomach. Not only was he sidelined, he also had to pay for school. Unlike many programs our athletic department won't pay a full scholarship for a student who is no longer eligible to play. Therefore, he had to return home and earn enough money to come back. I am pleased to report that a year later Guasco was back in school and working toward his engineering degree. Not without one more obstacle to overcome.

Guasco contacted me in the spring after I was fired to inquire about returning to school, so I contacted UMKC's director of compliance. When she told me the new administration would not approve the payment of his tuition, I called Jeffrey Flanagan, a columnist for *The Kansas City Star*. He followed up with a call to the new athletics director about Guasco. Surprisingly, the next day Guasco received a message stating UMKC would pay for his tuition. Thank you, Mr. Flanagan, and the power of the press for your assistance.

That same year we lost Dee Ayuba, an all-conference performer the previous year, to a torn ACL. He did not return to full strength until late January. Thinking of the impact of those two players, UMKC created a schedule that prepared us to win the league. The 'Roos had road games in the Great Alaska Shootout, Maryland, Arkansas, Wichita State and Northern Iowa. Earlier in the book I told you about the importance of scheduling at the low to mid-level. Well, I blew it.

That summer we had lost a guarantee game with Minnesota. Plus, to avoid being forced to play at K-State without a return game by my AD, I scheduled a game with Maryland. I felt our fans could use a couple more years to savor our previous win over K-State and a home game in the future. I know I wanted to.

The contract negotiations with Maryland were hampered by a deadline imposed by my AD In the end Maryland's businessperson got it done in more ways than one. In our last conversation before the contract was signed I asked for a photographer to be at the game. He undoubtedly thought I wanted a team picture in their new arena, but I asked to have a photograph of me in front of my wife's Hall of Fame plaque in the arena. I mentioned earlier she was an All-American lacrosse player with the Terrapins. He didn't flinch. In fact, he said they've had stranger requests. I wonder what they were.

We played the game at the end of a four-game swing that saw us take on four ranked teams. We ended up losing the game by more than six touchdowns. I appreciated it when Gary Williams yelled at one of his players for hitting a trey at the buzzer. He showed a lot of class. Boy, I hope my wife liked her picture!

The schedule in my last year was a product of too many cooks in the kitchen. For some reason my AD and assistant AD got involved, neither of whom had experience in that area. But they had plenty of opinions. I understood the delicacies of scheduling, especially with a young team. However, with their micro-managing I was forced to make some bad decisions. Besides the four ranked teams that provided us big paydays, I scheduled a home-and-home series with Utah Valley. I could have scheduled a game with Denver, which had won four games, but instead we played a non-conference team twice that had won 20 games. Not too smart.

Finally, we wore ourselves out early by playing too many road games. At one point we were on the road for 17 out of 26 days. NBA teams didn't even do that. My sole consolation was an abundance of frequent flyer miles. It wasn't worth it.

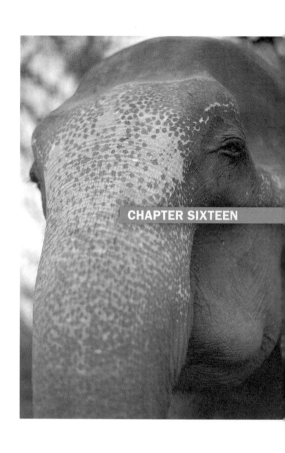

CHAPTER SIXTEEN

The Circus, Wal-Mart and Larry the Cable Guy

For too many years I have been at schools where I had no control over the practice or playing facility. And I don't mean sharing time with the women's team. I was very lucky when it came to women's basketball coaches. All of them were very agreeable about practice times. Maybe because we were in the same boat.

Unfortunately, I did not have the same relationships with intramural and facility directors. At UNF one practice was cancelled due to a flag football game. It was raining outside so they moved the intramural championship inside. They even asked me if I wanted to officiate. I declined! At St. Francis one was due to an intramural floor hockey game, one I ended up playing in. Our team won. But UMKC was the topper. We were shut out one week because of free play by the patrons. The recreation department had outside members who were placed on the schedule first. That's right. It was an outside group that got first choice. (I made sure I got the request in earlier next time.) In the meantime we went across the street to the gym at Rockhurst University. Do you think that ever happened to Lute Olson?

In the matter of home games, a big corporation played a role. Wal-Mart headquarters are located in Arkansas, but their company's annual convention is a big moneymaker for Kansas City. It is held in Municipal Auditorium, which meant every year from mid-January to mid-February—the heart of our league schedule—we were forced to move our home court. Of the 45 home conference games played during my tenure, only 28 were played at Municipal Auditorium. Nine were played at the larger and more cavernous Kemper Arena and eight at Hale Arena, which is adjacent to Kemper. Moving around did not help us gain any home court advantage. It usually meant only one practice in the facility before each weekday game due to classes. The visiting team usually had two. Before the home game against Western Illinois, neither team had practiced in the facility because of a concert by Larry the Cable Guy. At least I got free tickets.

Hale Arena was home to the American Royal, a traditional livestock show in Kansas City. The arena bowl is primarily used for rodeo events. Hale was the third option if Kemper was occupied. I remember the first time we played at Hale, when I was the assistant under Demopoulos. The head coach was trying to be hospitable so he gave the visitors the big locker room. We changed in one room then moved to another for pre- and post-game meetings. After the game while listening to the head coach address the team, a distinct odor wafted through my nostrils. It smelled like sewage. Looking down from where I stood I noticed I was on a grate. Under it was leftover cow dung. At that moment I realized we were in the room where they hose off the animals before they go out for the rodeo. Somebody forgot to flush! When I got the head coaching job the following year, I made sure we were never in the cow room again.

CHAPTER SEVENTEEN

Medical Training on the Job

Most coaches go through the normal injuries to knees, ankles and shoulders throughout their careers. I am no exception. A good trainer is a must. I have been blessed to have a number of good ones. One night in a game at Missouri State I noticed one of my players, Will Palmer, looking sluggish. He wasn't the quickest player on the court, but he sure looked like he lost a step. When I questioned him at halftime, he said the trainer gave him a muscle relaxer at the pre-game meal. The trainer told him it wouldn't affect him until after the game. I begged to differ.

In the last six years I had two players come down with appendicitis during the season and another develop a blood clot near his heart. In the case of the latter, it turned out he had a rib pressing on a vein. He had it removed by a surgeon in St. Louis and missed the whole season. He was never the same.

Medical problems were not always limited to the physical. I had one player share with me that his uncle abused him. Another came to me about parental abuse and demons he said that talked to him. Those were way beyond my psychiatric training, so I sent them to a sports psychologist. In the end the psychologist helped them through some tough times. When recruiting a player you never know how they'll turn out. Regardless of their ability I always believed it was my responsibility to help them grow on and off the court.

CHAPTER EIGHTEEN

Backpack of Life

For 25 years I chased the dream of cutting down the nets and hoisting the championship trophy. I grew up during a time when *Wide World of Sports* was must-see TV each weekend. Watching the opening highlights in which the "thrill of victory" and "agony of defeat" flashed on my television screen, I fantasized about becoming the featured character in the "thrill" of a victory shot. After all, "the agony of defeat" shot was a fellow Croatian who unfortunately fell off the ski jump platform. I thought a shot of me could help balance the scales.

The lessons I learned while on this journey molded me and might help you as well. As I tell kids all the time, "It's okay to have your head in the clouds as long as your feet are planted on the ground and headed in the right direction." I would like to share some of those lessons with you.

Every day you send your child to school or you head to work with a backpack full of the essentials – books, papers, pens, calculators et al – to learn, improve and get the job done. I wonder whether those backpacks contain the three most important pieces to success: the wishbone, backbone, and funnybone. It is important to have all three.

First let's talk about the wishbone: You must have a dream. Without a properly developed wishbone, you will never be able to reach your potential. You must have a dream. Those who don't will perish. I know that sounds intense, but try living a purposeful life without a sense of hope and ability to dream.

From the time I was an eighth grader I dreamed about becoming a head basketball coach at the Division I level. I really visualized it happening. I used to get so excited the hairs on the back of my neck stood up. That's how you must approach your dream before it turns into a goal. You have to taste it, touch it and feel it in your soul.

That's why each year I began our first practice by having the players sit on the floor with their eyes closed. I wanted them to visualize themselves playing a key role in winning a championship. Not an easy thing to do if players attend schools that never accomplished that. We would talk about creating our own tradition. Then I would play an audio tape created by radio play-by-play announcers. It started with my first head coaching job at St. Francis – Todd Ant made the tape – and it continued at UMKC with the since-departed radio guy Danny Clinkscale. Todd was also kind enough to do the tapes when I was at North Florida and Millersville.

The tape took the players through the final minutes of a championship game. The game-winner took on different forms depending on the year. One year it might be a defensive stop, another a last-second shot. As the final horn went off you cold hear the crowd scream and excitement fill the gym. As the band played you could cut the emotion with a knife. Then we would march to one end of the floor and cut down the nets to celebrate the victory. We did the same thing at the end of the year, but added a video of each player performing to his potential in the areas needed most. That sent everybody into the tourney with a huge jolt of confidence.

When you carry that type of visualization into the rest of your life, magic will happen. The truth is you become what you think about the majority of the time. Or in a manner of speaking, you don't always get what you want, but get what you expect.

The second bone I have found useful on my journey is the backbone. Without that your wishbone becomes just a wish with no chance of becoming true. As my father said, "If you don't stand for something, you will fall for anything."

Your backbone gives you the ability to turn adversity into advantage. I should know. I have had a lot of practice at dealing with adversity. But don't take my word for it. I am going to give you a little quiz:

Name the coach who had a senior stand up at the season-ending banquet and talk about how the coach ruined his career. That same coach had a star player publicly criticize his coaching in the newspaper and had two different players arrested for drugs while playing for him. No, it wasn't me. It was the legendary UCLA coach John Wooden. And despite those obstacles he managed to win 11 national championships. He's revered today as a coach who molded fine young men.

There are times when it might be easy to cut corners. I could have kept my leading scorer at UNF and, in all likelihood, won a few more games, but you must have a set of principles that guide you. Mine were imbedded by my parents and coaches, and for that I am thankful. There were certainly times while I was coaching at UMKC when we struggled. Like starting 0-7 in 2004-05. It would have been easy to pack it in and start believing what my critics were saying. But, I thought about the mailman and whether he worried so much about every barking dog. If he did, the mail would never get delivered. So I just kept working and believing. It ended up producing one of the best years in UMKC history.

Last, but certainly not least, is the funnybone. Coaching basketball taught me the importance of learning to laugh. The ability to laugh at yourself is a key to getting through some of the valleys inevitably faced in the course of competition. You find yourself in some awkward positions when you are dealing with stress and emotion. I know I did.

While at the University of North Florida I got so frustrated during a game that I put my fist through the portable chalkboard. My point was made and the team was riveted, but the moment was lost when I couldn't get my hand detached from the chalkboard. So much for the point of emphasis. I guess the point at that time was not punching an object unless it's solid. Another time I picked up a trash can and threw it across the locker room. I thought it was empty. Unfortunately, it was full of cups and orange peels. Quite a mess. I spent the next 30 minutes cleaning it up so the janitor wouldn't be upset.

The importance of laughter was not lost on the late Jim Valvano as he so aptly put what he considered a full day. His words: "If you spend each day in thought and are moved emotionally to both tears and laughter, then you have lived a full day." I couldn't agree more! Through the course of my career I have found the benefit of laughter in a tough situation and have been brought to tears by both disappointing losses and joyous victories. I actually cried when I watched Marcos Santos walk across the stage with a diploma in hand. Of course my daughter Kailey says my emotion is caused by watching too many chick flicks.

Communication has also been a key to my climb through the coaching ranks. Whether teaching, selling or managing people, communication is vital to success. I have worked for athletics directors who let you know exactly where you stood at all times. Carlo Tromontozzi at St. Francis was the best in my experience. There were no e-mails or memos. It was all face-to-face communication. And with his fiery Italian personality there were times when we went face-to-face. One time I left the Terriers' sports information director, Patrick Horne, at the gym following a game against Wright State University. Tired of waiting and frustrated by the loss, I told the bus driver to take us back to the hotel, then go back and pick him up. When we returned to New York, Tromontozzi made it clear that I should never do that again. I never did.

Another lesson I learned about communication was taught to me by Kailey when she was nine months old. I came home from practice one day, and Sandy was in the kitchen feeding her baby food. Well, she was trying. The food was on the floor, splashed against the wall, and practically covering my wife. But nothing was in the kid. So I bullied my way into the situation and told my wife I would take care of the feeding.

**My last Final Four as a head coach with Colin, Devin and some close friends.
L-R: Gary Edwards, Colin, Devin, Me, Joe Cantefeo, Todd Ant, Bob Valvano.**

My first mistake.

As she walked out I blew my whistle to get my daughers attention. With her eyes riveted on me, she clamped her mouth shut. At nine months she made the decision not to eat. I did what a lot of parents do. I took three spoonfuls and then offered her a spoonful. She refused and gave me a look like, "If you want it that bad, you eat it."

After getting her mouth open I shoved three spoonfuls in. She then made her second decision. Die by holding her breath instead of swallowing. I told her I didn't care. I had two other children, as if she could understand my ranting. Then, after what seemed like five minutes, she caught me with my guard down and spit it out. Just then my wife walked in and gave me a look as if to say, "Yeah, a big time coach and you can't even get your daughter to eat baby food." I then told my wife it was obvious. "Kailey didn't like the green stuff. Feed her the orange stuff." And then I humbly walked out of the kitchen. My daughter taught me a valuable lesson on communication that day. To this day I still don't know how my wife got her to eat the green stuff.

CHAPTER NINETEEN

It's About Relationships

It has been a wonderful journey the past 25 years, filled with plenty of highs and lows. I have driven more than a million miles in search of the next great player. I even learned how to drive with my knees while eating my dinner. That drove my assistants nuts, but it meant moving on instead of stopping. Ask me about the location of any landmark in a major city and I can tell you as long as you tell me the closest high school.

During my journey to ten different colleges in nine different states, I have lived in 13 different houses or apartments. My oldest son Colin was born in Brooklyn while my other two children, Devin and Kailey, were born in Jacksonville, Florida. In fact, Colin attended seven schools in 12 years.

Coaching at so many different colleges gave me the opportunity to work at both private and public schools. Some big, some small and most without football. Most were commuter schools. The only common thread was all were rebuilding projects. I worked for seven different head coaches in nine years as an assistant. I am pleased to say that I am still friends with all of them to this day. That makes me proud. Also, I have worked for eight different athletics directors in 16 years as a head coach. I am still working on those relationships.

Through it all the one driving force has been the players. I have always tried to make an impact on their lives. Many of them went on to play professionally, mostly overseas. Others have become ministers, lawyers, engineers, politicians and teachers. I had one player become a state highway patrolman. That's good. I may need to get out of another speeding ticket. However, the ones who make me extremely proud are those who became coaches. Those are the ones I feel like I had a direct impact on.

As I look back, the most important part of the journey has been the relationships along the way. To this day my best feeling is when a former player calls to tell me about a new job or a new baby. It means I have another pair of baby sneakers to send.

One of the best calls I received came in March 2007. It was from Ricky Melendez, one of the first players I recruited. He told me that

With my first recruit, Ricky Melendez, and high school teammate, Dino Pelusi, at our induction ceremony at the Lorian Sports Hall of Fame. Who says life doesn't come full circle?

he was going to be inducted into the Lorain Sports Hall of Fame and wanted me to be there. I said there was no other place I wanted to be that day. I sounded like a proud father talking to his son.

On May 4, 2007, life seemed to come full circle. The day Ricky was inducted into the Lorain Sport Hall of Fame, I was, too. A couple nights after Ricky told me his good news, I received a call about my induction.

As I sat at the head table next to Ricky, I knew the journey had all been worthwhile. The same pride I had in my eyes for Ricky I could see in my father's eyes. It was one of the best moments of my life.

The game of basketball has taken me to so many places over the last 25 years. I have had the opportunity to live in big cities and small towns. I have met and worked with hundreds of tremendous people from all walks of life. Not bad for a kid from a steel mill town in Ohio. Maybe it was fate that one of my last acts on the basketball journey was held back home. Who knows?

As I later reflected on the beach in Ocean City, Maryland, I knew I had reached a fork in the road. But as Yogi Berra said, "When you come to a fork in the road, take it." That's what I told myself I would do. You never know where it may take you.

Epilogue

More than a year has passed since my exit from the coaching world. I wish I can say I miss it, but I don't. Sure there are aspects I miss—the camaraderie of the coaches and players, the preparation and practice time, the competition of a big game. But I don't miss the business part and all the non-basketball duties related to coaching.

Since leaving coaching I was hired as an analyst on the Big Ten television network. I really appreciate Tim Sutton, the coordinating producer of live events, taking a chance on me and providing assistance. My year there helped me land a package of games on ESPN.

My first game was a non-conference game at Michigan between the Wolverines and Radford. Man, do I remember being in the shoes of Radford coach Brad Greenberg. After the Wolverines won the game handily, I'll never forget the look on Greenberg's face when I bumped into him in the lobby. I don't care how much money was collected for the athletic coffers at Radford. It doesn't erase the pain of a double digit loss. Greenberg was already trying to figure out how to convince his kids to wipe away the memory of that game and think ahead to their game with Eastern Michigan in 48 hours. It was like a flashback to what I'd been doing not long before. I didn't miss that part at all. In fact I hated tough guarantee game losses. But, instead of agonizing over bus departures and fast food joints, the only thing I had to do that night was decide where to eat dinner. And, believe me, I had a better piece of mind comfortably dining that night.

Thank goodness I worked with broadcast veteran Roger Twibell. From working with ABC Sports and ESPN, he knew how to put me at ease. I found that the preparation is similar to a coach. But the big difference is second-guessing another coach as opposed to being second-guessed. I must admit I enjoyed it. No loss to add to my ledger and all my plays worked to perfection!

While interviewing Michigan coach John Beilein, we reminisced about the time I beat him out for the University of North Florida job. It turned out to be a break for him because the following year he moved on to the Division I level at Canisius University. It was a big step for him en route to a successful and lucrative coaching career.

I also threw myself into the acting profession after taking acting lessons from Andy Garrison at the Actor Training Studio in Kansas City. A tremendous teacher, Andy really helped me improve my new craft. Subsequently, I was cast in *The Drive* as the chief of the Secret Service. Plus, I was cast in a couple of movies as an FBI Agent and a police detective. I guess the authoritative look of a coach can be used in other professions. I even got to play a football coach on *Friday Night Lights*. Check your local DVD racks, too, for *Sisters Four* and *Formosa Betrayed*.

Two things I learned while pursuing my new careers—I became myopic over how people view their work, and my last name is meaningless.

My myopia developed as my coaching career continued. Throughout that part of my life, I was constantly asked by aspiring young people what they needed do to get into the profession. My first response was always that you really have to love it. I repeated that so often that I began to believe that coaching was the only profession where you had to absolutely love it to be successful. I later found out from talking with professionals in the broadcasting and acting fields that they feel the same way about their chosen endeavor. Now that I have worked in these professions since leaving coaching, I realize they are 100 percent correct. You really do have to love what you're doing. Thank goodness I'm doing something I love again. How lucky I am!

Second, I learned a different way to introduce myself. In business and coaching you always introduced yourself by saying your first and last name. However, as an actor, your first name is sufficient. It will take a while for me to get used to that difference. And I still don't understand why only your first name is important. My theory is that many actors have changed their names and can't remember their real last name.

Another area I explored is the business of professional speaking. Having given so many speeches over the years as part of my public relations duties, it's natural. My topic is turning adversity into an advantage. Through the years I certainly had plenty of practice at that. It also gives me an opportunity to give back with hopes of helping people by providing a lift through inspiration.

If I told you that I didn't notice how UMKC's basketball team performed since my departure from the program, I'd be lying. I still live in the Kansas City area, so I can't help but to see some of the newspaper and television coverage. Besides, I still had players on the team I felt responsible for and hoped that they would do well.

The team, though it returned three starters, went 11-21 overall and 6-12 in The Summit League. UMKC's overall record was worse than my last season (12-20). Its conference record was the worst since going 3-11 in 1998-99, two years before I was hired as an assistant there under Dean Demopoulos. Individually, Tim Blackwell had a good senior season after struggling in his junior year. I was happy for him. Also, Dane Brumagin was named all-conference and showed great maturation in his junior year. Dane's my last link to the program.

When the Kangaroos established a school record in 2005 for 12 conference wins, their best since joining the league, there was a stretch of four home games—from Feb. 5 to Feb. 22—when the atmosphere at Municipal Auditorium was phenomenal. In three of the four home games during that stretch, the 'Roos drew more than 6,500 fans. All three games rank in UMKC's top-10 list for best crowds. Everything UMKC set out to do when it made a commitment to play Division I basketball beginning in December, 1987, appeared to be close to reality. It wasn't the stature of Marquette or DePaul as a major municipal university athletic program. But, as I hoped, it started to carve its own niche in the heart of Big 12 country.

I'd like to think my coaches and I assembled an exciting team dotted with local players that a city rich with college basketball tradition appreciated. Unfortunately, when the team rebuilds, so does the university with its fan base. The attendance took a tumble in the 2007-08 season. Only once did the 'Roos top the 3,000 mark in attendance.

But these days that's the least of my concerns. As I have in my life, UMKC has turned the page.

Graduation day for Colin. Due to my many job changes, Colin went to seven different schools in four states. Left to right: Kailey, Colin, Sandy, Devin, me